O.S. NOCK'S
Railway Reminiscences
of the
Interwar Years

O.S.NOCK'S
Railway
Reminiscences
of the
Interwar Years

LONDON
IAN ALLAN LTD

First published 1980

ISBN 0 7110 1042 0

Published by Ian Allan Ltd, Shepperton, Surrey;
and printed by Ian Allan Printing Ltd at their works
at Coombelands in
Runnymede, England

Contents

Preface

The 20-year period between the two world wars marked the culmination of steam locomotive development all over the world. It is true that the history of its evolution was not quite completed in 1939, and that certain unorthodox designs were to come at the end of the war; but the basic practice of Chapelon, Gresley and Stanier, of the American articulateds for fast main line work, and of the Beyer-Garratt was fully established. All in all, the period between the wars was an exciting and colourful era, despite increasing standardisation of designs in Great Britain, on account of Grouping. But equally the period was enlivened by the frequent calls made upon the locomotives of that legendary age before 1914 for fast and heavy work, and by the success they achieved in doing it.

At the beginning of this interwar period I was a schoolboy of 14 possessed of my first camera and a burning enthusiasm for railways that dates back to my cradle. At the end of it I had advanced sufficiently in my profession to have been elected a chartered mechanical engineer, and to have become a full member of the Institution of Railway Signal Engineers, of which I ultimately became President. Apart from my ordinary daily work my interest in railways was, from the very beginning of this interwar period, always twofold — photography, and the study of train running, inspired by my regular study of *The Railway Magazine*. Later my earliest amateur enthusiasm became strengthened by an increasing professional awareness of the engineering background to what I saw.

Although it was not long before my signalling work was involved with railways in many parts of the world, as a designer, and thus an 'indoor' man, I did not have to travel far afield. By the outbreak of war, in 1939, my journeys had not taken me further than France, Holland, and the whole of Ireland. Nevertheless, within those parameters, and of course the entire length and breadth of Great Britain I saw a great deal, and the present book is a series of informal essays on the more interesting aspects of the interwar scene, illustrated entirely by my own photographs.

A very long time ago I did all my own processing in a dark room improvised in my parents' home in Barrow. The window screen that I rigged up in the bathroom was a useful prototype for the black-out screens I made for our Chippenham house during World War II. But increasing calls on my spare time and the move to a new family home at Bushey got me somewhat disorganised, and I realised that the time had come when I should have to use some D&P firm. The early results were disastrous. It was perhaps too much to expect that commercial photographers would pay any heed to the finer points of printing railway negatives, which, as all those who practise the art know only too well, often needs a certain amount of titivating to get ideal prints. For a month or so I was despondent, vacillating between various local chemists, with post-mortems that usually ended in slanging matches, and a jury rigged 'dark room' in the scullery of our new home, which was more than once burst into, by a particularly brainless resident maid!

Then one day, for some reason I cannot now recall, a copy was wanted of an old, and very faded family portrait. In my lunch hour peregrinations around the Kings Cross area I had noticed a small window in the Pentonville Road showing portraits, and without really much hope I called in. The 'shop' was no more than a counter at the foot of a flight of stairs; but a pleasant young lady came down in answer to my ring, took a searching look at that old print, and thought she could do something with it. I went back in about a week's time and witnessed a miracle. By the most skilful treatment that old portrait had been verily brought back to life again. The family were delighted, but already my thoughts were beginning to run in a different direction: would this obviously expert young lady be prepared to try her hand with locomotives?

After some initial hesitation she agreed to have a go. We ran a few trial heats, but in a remarkably short time she got the message, and so, for the last six years of peace she did all my D&P work. I can never cease to be grateful to Elsie Lowman. It was not only a matter of locomotives and trains. She brought out the best in pictures I had taken of signalling installations, marshalling yards and colliery plants, and she prepared albums of beautiful enlargements for Westinghouse to present to customers. Today, many of the reproductions in this book are from prints she made more than 40 years ago, and they are as crisp, and free from stains and fading as the day she made them.

The photographs used in this book however, were in many cases taken more than 55 years ago, and it would be surprising if some of the film negatives were not showing some deterioration. In making prints for reproduction I am much indebted to Mr G. Woodgate of Bromhead (Bristol) Ltd for the care and skill he has shown in coaxing something near to pristine quality out of some of these older efforts of mine.

In writing this book, and in choosing the pictures I realise how fortunate I have been in the permission I had from the various railways to roam the lineside and photograph at will, and in later years to ride on the footplate of so many different locomotives. My grateful thanks are due to all who helped me so much. I am no less grateful to my father and mother who encouraged so wholeheartedly my early interest in railways, who bought my first cameras, and financed my early expeditions. In later years Olivia, my wife, herself at one time on the London and North Eastern Railway, has been my constant companion on railway travels, and as secretary and keen critic of all my literary work, a never failing tower of strength to me.

Twenty Eight,
High Bannerdown,
Batheaston,   *O. S. Nock,*
Bath.   *September 1979*

1
The Northern Scene

At the end of the war, a schoolboy of 14, I was travelling three times a year in each direction between Barrow-in-Furness and Giggleswick by the Furness and Midland Railways, with a sight of the London and North Western in the often lengthy connecting time at Carnforth. Though the eastward journeys in January, April and September were naturally invested with the gloom inevitable in the transition from home comforts to the rigours of boarding school life the interest of the railway journey did much to soften the pangs of parting, especially as the time at Carnforth was one that included much first class activity on the LNWR main line. In recalling those early journeys, however, the actual travelling, on the Furness and on the Midland, included much that was of historic interest.

Among the denizens of Barrow in those days the Furness Railway was regarded as something of a sluggard, as good for the 'knock' of a local humorist as the Brighton and the South Eastern of 19th century England were for E. L. Ahrons. But on reflection, although the overall times between Carnforth and Barrow were not exactly meteoric the company had done a mighty job of transportation in the war, and passenger trains did not have first priority. The trains I used called at all stations between Barrow and Carnforth, and were usually hauled by the 6ft 6in Pettigrew 4-4-0s, one of the most handsome engines of the type ever to run. They were hardly ideal for working a heavy stopping train, particularly over such gradients as those leading up to Lindal Moor. But they were always kept in beautiful condition. At the end of each term we boys could not get away from school fast enough, and there was a Leeds to Morecambe train that called at Giggleswick at 7.56am. We had to change at Wennington, and that meant waiting for a short shuttle train to arrive from Carnforth, usually hauled by a Johnson 0-4-4T engine. The Furness train with which this connected was sometimes hauled by a 0-6-2T engine; but although having the apparent advantage of six-coupled wheels progress never seemed to be so good as when we had a Pettigrew 4-4-0.

In those school days I cannot remember being hauled by one of the larger Pettigrew 4-4-0s, having 6ft diameter coupled wheels. One of these usually took the midday train from Barrow, which was the nearest approach to an express the Furness had in the up direction at that time, and conveyed a through carriage for Euston. Naturally, at the beginning of the school term I, and the other Barrovians bound for Giggleswick, took the latest train possible, and this was an 'all-stations' leaving Barrow about 5pm. We used to reckon 1½ hours for the run, but on referring to the contemporary timetable I find that the actual allowance was 1hr 20min. This was quite commendable for a run of 28½ miles including nine intermediate stops; but I recall to this day that the 4-4-0 engines, which were then about 20 years old, and non-superheated, made heavy weather of the severely uphill starts from Furness Abbey and Dalton. Our home was near to the former station, and we normally used it in preference to Barrow Central.

Of the line north of Barrow I have less emotional experiences, because these were entirely connected with summer holiday expeditions, chiefly to Coniston, Ravenglass and Seascale. The Pettigrew 4-4-2Ts worked on the Coniston branch, and also on that from Ulverston to Lakeside (Windermere); but so far as tank engines were concerned, the 0-6-2Ts used to work the 'specials' run during the latter part of the war for munition workers in the shell-shop at Vickers' Works in Barrow. These trains, composed of LNWR six-wheeled stock, and painted chocolate brown all over ran from a single tracked line in Island Road, between two sections of the works. This connected with the so-called Dock line, and by a triangle junction at Salthouse had direct connections to both north and south of Barrow for these special trains.

In the last year I was travelling to and from Giggleswick the large 'Baltic' tanks took the road, though it was not until some years later that I had a trip behind one of them. When W. F. Pettigrew retired from the post of Locomotive, Carriage and Wagon Superintendent, in 1918, the Civil Engineer, D. L. Rutherford, was given charge of the locomotive department in addition to his former duties, and E. Sharples, became assistant for all mechanical engineering matters. This change has led to the statement sometimes made that Rutherford *designed* the big 4-6-4Ts that went into traffic in 1920. My parents knew both Rutherford and Sharples, and at dinner one night in our home the latter put the matter succinctly: 'Rutherford said he wanted a 4-6-4 so we had to design one'. I remember asking Sharples why the new engines were not superheated, and he laughingly replied: 'Oh, we can't afford superheaters on our short runs'. As a budding young engineer, steeped in the descriptions of new locomotives in *The Railway Magazine* I remember thinking this very strange; but in later years I came to know how even a man in so pre-eminent a position as C. J. Bowen Cooke, when first becoming Chief Mechanical Engineer of the LNWR, had to go cap-in-hand to the top management to obtain authority to spend the extra money, on a superheated version of the 'Precursors'. Even then his authority at first extended to only one engine until the almost phenomenal saving in coal over a non-superheated engine was demonstrated.

The Furness 4-6-4Ts were tremendously impressive to look upon. I must confess that until they came upon the scene, as a youngster I had tended to look upon the line as something of a backwater: attractive certainly in the distinctive colouring of the engines, and in the delightful country it served, but very small beer compared to the North Western and the Midland. But the big new engines added a new dimension to the Furness scene, and in school holidays I frequently found myself at the lineside between Furness Abbey and Roose looking out for them. On the far side of the short tunnel at Furness Abbey station there is a level crossing from which an attractive footpath walk led through some woodland beside the railway, and by some means I contrived that the time-honoured Sunday morning walk which we always took *en famille* frequently led that way! Teenage impressions apart however, the new 4-6-4Ts were ideal engines for the heavy stopping trains, and made short work of getting away from stations like Furness Abbey, Dalton, or from Ulverston in the down direction, where there were stiff gradients.

In contrast to the quiet deliberation of passenger train working on the Furness line, all was dash and bustle on the North Western side at Carnforth. While we waited for the Midland train to take us on to Giggleswick no fewer than three major down trains came through. The first was the ever-famous 'Corridor' then leaving Euston at 1pm. Although it was then much decelerated from its prewar standards of speed it used to sweep through Carnforth in most impressive style, always hauled by a 'Claughton' class 4-6-0. Two occasions that I remember were when *J. A. F. Aspinall* was on the job, and another when the load was heavy enough to require piloting and No 155 *I. T. Williams* was assisted by a 'Jumbo' No 1481 *Newton*. The former engine was later renamed *Sir Thomas Williams*, when the gentleman concerned, General Manager of the LNWR was knighted. The other two down trains that passed through during our connectional interval were a heavy express parcels, again usually 'Claughton' hauled, and the evening Liverpool and Manchester 'Scotsman', which brought the through carriages for Barrow and Whitehaven that had come down from Euston on the 'Corridor' as far as Crewe. The Liverpool and Manchester train was usually very heavy and I have seen it worked by two 'Prince of Wales' class 4-6-0s.

The working at Carnforth only served to whet my appetite for more, and in the summer of 1921 when I was leaving school, and had reached a certain standard as a medium distance cyclist I persuaded my parents to let me ride from Barrow to the North Western main line at Oxenholme, and points north. I studied my father's Ordnance Survey maps, and found that a road ran adjacent to that portion of the Grayrigg bank where the line is running almost due east and west. This I judged would give me a good sun position on the up side of the railway, but I had no idea what points of vantage would be available. Again from the map I saw that there was a relatively direct road, only 11 miles long from Newby Bridge to Kendal, but when I tried it in the Easter holidays of 1921 it proved terribly hilly, crossing Gummer's How, with a marvellous view over Windermere, at an altitude of 752ft. On subsequent trips I took the longer, but much easier route through Lindale and across the marshes to Levens Bridge, there joining the main road to Carlisle.

In the Easter holidays there was a coal strike on, but although getting home from school had been fraught with uncertainties it did not occur to me that the LNWR main line services would be affected. Yet so it was, and my first expedition to the Grayrigg bank produced somewhat scanty results. I found excellent view points near Hay Fell box, but a long vigil yielded no more than two down freights, one hauled by a 19-inch 4-6-0 and the other by one of the ex-ROD GCR type 2-8-0s (later LNER Class 04) of which the LNWR had taken a number, temporarily. But I waited in vain for any of the up midday group of expresses, and as time went on I had to retrace my steps to Oxenholme, in the hopes of seeing something there. While in transit, but too far from the line to identify its engines there came a lengthy up express, drifting without steam down the bank, headed by a 'Jumbo' and a 'Prince of Wales'. But I had one rich reward when the down morning 'Scotsman', then 9.30am ex-Euston, came thundering through headed by none other than the war memorial engine No 1914 *Patriot*. That engine had only just ended her long stint on the down 'Corridor', daily from Euston to Crewe and back; she was an unusual visitor on the Northern Division.

The coal strike dragged on into the early summer, and when I went to sit for the London Matriculation examination at Birmingham University train services were still much attenuated. The 9.30am from Euston, normally non-stop from Crewe to Carlisle in the good time of 165min having regard to its rarely having less than 14 on — was calling at Preston to pick up Liverpool and Manchester passengers.

With 'Claughtons' regularly on the job piloting was rare, south of Oxenholme at any rate. On that Easter holiday occasion *Patriot* had taken her big load up Grayrigg bank without help. On our return from Birmingham my mother and I travelled by the 'Scotsman' from Crewe to Preston, and although it was before I had begun regularly timing I recall that 'Claughton' No 2035, then unnamed, gave us a fast run, albeit 'enjoyed' from a seat on my suitcase in the corridor!

With industrial relations returning to normal in the late summer the LNWR in company with some of the other major railways made important accelerations of passenger train services in the October timetables of 1921, one outcome of which was the division of the morning Anglo-Scottish expresses at Crewe. Within my cycling time from Barrow there were no fewer than seven expresses on the Grayrigg bank, three down and four up. The latter group came first: 10am Edinburgh-Euston; 10am Glasgow-Euston; 10.10am Glasgow-Liverpool and Manchester; Up Aberdeen, due in Euston 7.30pm.

Then came the down midday Liverpool and Manchester 'Scotch', sometimes quaintly referred to by local railwaymen as 'The Yorkshireman'! The exciting sequence was completed by the two portions of the 10am from Euston, which from October 1921 had taken up its historic departure time, instead of the wartime 9.30am.

Although by that time my 'seat of learning' had changed from Giggleswick to South Kensington I still enjoyed long holidays, and at Eastertide 1922 I was up at Hay Fell once again. Of the seven expresses the two Liverpool and Manchesters were hauled by 'Prince of Wales' 4-6-0s, but all the rest had 'Claughtons'. The two sections of the down 10am were both providing spectacular smoke effects, which gave me what were probably my best shots of LNWR engines in action. The first of the two trains, hauled by No 163 *Holland Hibbert* was making a tremendously vigorous ascent, with splendid acoustic effects. It was long before the days of tape recorders, and other sound recordings of train noises; but the roar of a beautifully tuned up 'Claughton' doing about 45mph up Grayrigg bank would have given sounds worthy to be played back over and over again.

I think however that my most productive day in the Westmorland fell country was in September 1923, when I had enough pocket money on hand to make the entire journey by train and go through to Tebay. I took the 9.15am from Barrow, as far as Grange-over-Sands, then the 'Kendal donkey' via Arnside and Heversham, to Oxenholme, and lastly the Carlisle semi-fast, I was out by the water troughs in time for the morning Liverpool and Manchester 'Scotsman'. On it a 'Jumbo' and a 'Claughton', *Countess* and *Lady Godiva* gave me a spectacular picture — still one of my favourites — and a rare ducking from the spray. By that time I had a walking permit, and went down as far as the approaches to Low Gill; but again it was the two portions of the 10am from Euston that provided the greatest thrills.

I was setting up my camera ready for the Glasgow portion when a local goods came trickling through, and sure enough it was not clear into the yard at Tebay when the express approached. Down the valley I could see that it was nearly brought to a stand at Dillicar signals. I saw also it was double headed. By the time they came through the rock cutting and on to the troughs the two engines were truly tearing into it, piling on every ounce of speed to charge Shap. I was surprised to see that the leading engine was a superheated 'Precursor' — by a coincidence the very last of the class to survive, No 643 *Sirocco*; but since the introduction in postwar years of so many new 'Princes' and 'Claughtons' the 4-4-0s were becoming rare birds on the Northern Division. The train engine was an unnamed

'Prince', No 198, quite a favourite on crack workings at that time. The Edinburgh and Aberdeen portion of the train had a clear run through, and to my delight the engine sweeping effortlessly past at about 65mph was the *Sir Gilbert Claughton*. I was to see this famous engine many times in later years, numbered 5900, painted Midland red, and stationed at Leeds; but the appearance was rather spoiled by the big ex-ROD tender, quite apart from the alien style of painting. That day, in September 1923, was the last time I went photographing up in the fells, until many years later.

Although none of the engines I saw that day were painted red there was evidence of change in that the Liverpool and Manchester 'Scotsman', that had preceded *Sirocco* and No 198 was hauled by a Hughes 4-cylinder 4-6-0. Having said that it is time I wrote of the Midland in my school days.

Of the 'Little North Western', and its continuation to Carnforth, so cherished today as one of the regular steam routes, my recollections are of the extraordinary variety of Midland motive power we had. The beautiful Johnson 2-4-0s were much in evidence, but there were also a few of the unrebuilt Johnson 4-4-0s stationed at Hellifield, and used for piloting on the Settle and Carlisle line. I remember once when the family were travelling east, bound eventually for Bridlington, being held up at Settle Junction to let the morning Leeds-Glasgow express go through, and a thrilling sight she was, hauled by one of the unrebuilt Johnson 4-4-0s and a 999 Class 4 4-0. The down Midland Scotch expresses always used to get away from Hellifield with tremendous gusto, making every use of the down grade to Settle Junction to pile on speed to charge 'The Long Drag'. The purists may tilt at my use of the word 'Scotch'; but in the Midland timetables, both in the books and on broadsheets pasted on station boards all Anglo-Scottish trains were labelled 'Scotch Express'. So, as far as the Midland is concerned 'Scotch' it is!

On the line to Carnforth we often had the rebuilt superheated Class 2 4-4-0s, and equally non-superheated rebuilds, and over the heavy gradients of the line double heading was frequent. Two of the Johnson 2-4-0s in tandem made a very pretty sight. I saw such a combination several times. At Giggleswick School we had a training run that took us over the high ground to the west of the school, down to a crossing of the railway, and then by another by-road past the station. Although strenuous training, for the annual Scarrig cross-country race was a first consideration I used to try and time things so that I was on that by-road when the afternoon train from Morecambe came up the bank from Clapham Junction, usually hauled by a Class 2 superheater rebuild. It was surprising what big loads were taken by the 2-4-0 engines in those far-off days. I remember one occasion when we were pounding up the 1 in 100 from a standing start on the grade at Giggleswick when a lady passenger, one of that ilk who talk in loud voices across a crowded non-corridor carriage, remarked to her husband: 'It strikes me we're going very slowly!' So we were, with a 2-4-0 hauling at least 200 tons of train. I also recall my housemaster once saying that the section from Giggleswick to Clapham Junction was the slowest five miles of railway he knew.

On the main line through Settle the 10 engines of the 999 class, had the principal express services practically to themselves, even though there were no more than 10 of them. It was only when postwar reconstruction of the timetables brought separate restaurant car trains for Glasgow and Edinburgh that the Class 2 superheater rebuilds came to some extent into the picture. The Edinburgh trains were mostly quite light, and could easily be managed. My recollection, however, is that many of the Midland engines at that time had lost much of their pristine glory of finish. The 999 class often looked rather shop-soiled, as also did some of the 2-4-0s working on the Carnforth and Morecambe trains. What I do recall, however, with much pleasure, is the truly splendid coaches in which we used to travel to and from school. The Clayton non-corridors, with their large windows, and attractive upholstery were a striking change from the Furness coaches, or — tell it not in Gath! — much of the LNWR stock passing through Carnforth at that time. But for us boys the change from Furness to Midland at Carnforth was one step nearer to the rigours of boarding school life, and we were not in the mood to appreciate the merits of the coaching stock.

I remember one beginning-of-term journey with three other boys from Furness line stations when the transit time at Carnforth had been unusually interesting to me, and I had lingered until almost the last minute on the North Western platforms. Eventually I found my schoolmates with a convivial party, bound for Leeds. The train was crowded, and they had just managed to save a seat for me, but the convivial party — two men and one woman — sought to make the last minutes of the school holidays as enjoyable as possible for us. Before we left Carnforth we were asked if we had plenty of cigarettes — a thrashing from the prefects if we were caught at school! — and my companions relaxed in a final 'puff'. There were others in the carriage, but this trio, in a very pleasant way monopolised the conversation. It was past 7 o'clock, and they were already in gala mood, looking forward to a *'glass of lemonade'* at Keighley. The time passed quickly, but there was no railway note taking on that trip.

I was unlucky in my photographs on the Midland in my last year at Giggleswick. With one film the dishes in the school dark room got mixed, and it went into the hypo first! On another occasion a suddenly granted half holiday for some special circumstance found me without film, and I had to be content with watching the morning Glasgow express come pounding up the bank past Stainforth, with the usual 999, and letting its progress register only in my memory. Then there was a time when I dared authority, school and otherwise, by climbing on to the embankment north of Settle station, and photographing the up 'Scotsman' a train usually hauled by a compound; but the result was miserable. So, alas, I have nothing to show pictorially for my sojourn near to such a grand line as the Settle and Carlisle. Having got as far as Grayrigg and Tebay on the North Western I explored the possibilities of a holiday expedition to the Midland via Tebay and the North Eastern line; but the train service was so sparse as to make it impossible in a day.

On one of my visits to Tebay I got an unexpected bonus, for there sitting in the bay platform at the head of a Darlington train was an immaculate Fletcher 901 class 2-4-0. This was actually the last of my early encounters with North Eastern locomotives, which had begun as early as 1919 at Bridlington. But in years just after World War I the Darlington-Tebay passenger service, usually consisting of three-coach non-corridor trains, was regularly worked by 2-4-0 engines, sometimes of the 'Tennant', or 1463 class, or otherwise by the 901 class originally of Fletcher design but rebuilt with Worsdell type boilers. My very first ride in a North Eastern train, from Leeds to Bridlington in 1919 had been behind a 'Tennant', but at that time there were not many of them left on the lines in the East Riding of Yorkshire. The most general power on the passenger trains between Leeds, Hull and Scarborough were the F and G class Worsdell 4-4-0s, though if one was lucky many other engines of 19th century vintage made occasional appearances.

During family holidays at Bridlington I found my way to a lane beside the sheds, and even a Box-Brownie camera proved a passport to invitations from the friendly enginemen to climb the fence, and on one memorable occasion to join them on the footplate. The engine that time was a J, 7ft 7in, 4-2-2 single, which class, strangely enough, were sometimes used on Scarborough trains from Bridlington, having to climb the severe gradients to Flamborough. I snapped No 1519 one day toiling up the bank with a 6-coach train, but the one I shall always hold in reverence is No 1522 on whose footplate I rode round the yard at Bridlington. It was the first time I had ever ridden an engine in steam, and I remember how surprised and a little shocked I was at the harshness of the motion. While the F class were the most frequent on the passenger trains the larger M and Q class 4-4-0s were occasional visitors to Bridlington. On the freights 0-6-0s of Class C predominated, though we got an occasional superheated 0-8-0 of Class T2. I do not remember, however, seeing any tank engines around Bridlington.

When visiting school friends in Leeds we cycled out to Arthington, and I saw the big 3-cylinder 4-4-4Ts of Class D on the Leeds-Harrogate residential trains, though my principal recollection of these latter is from a holiday at Whitby in 1922. Again I was favoured with lineside walking permits, but I was disappointed in the lack of variety of engine power in that area, despite the intersection of two distinct lines. There were then no passenger tender engines stationed at Whitby. The 4-4-0s of Classes F and R worked in from York, but the locals on the line to Pickering were worked by Class O 0-4-4T engines. When walking round the shed yard rather disconsolately one day I secured a supreme 'cop', the historic significance of which I did not appreciate in the least until some years later. This was 0-6-0 No 1275, one of the very last of the celebrated Stockton and Darlington long-boilered goods — the engine, in fact, that was subsequently restored to its original condition, ran in the Railway Centenary pageant of 1925, and is now in the North Road Museum at Darlington.

On the coastal route from Scarborough to Saltburn the Wilson Worsdell 4-6-2Ts of Class W had the passenger service nearly to themselves. They were slow cumbersome things: '. . . more like dredgers than engines', as one driver pungently expressed it! But there was a mid-afternoon train on which a Darlington engine used to work through to Whitby West Cliff, and then change trains with a 4-6-2 that had come up from Scarborough; and this job was worked by a 4-4-4T of Class D. Although the wheel arrangement was far from ideal on so hilly a route, adhesion wise, the 4-4-4Ts were far superior as vehicles, and as the trains usually did not consist of more than four non-corridor coaches the loading did not trouble them. Those 4-4-4Ts were just as popular with their crews as the 4-6-2s were disliked.

Although those years just after World War I lay well before the time of decline in railway travel it is surprising how slow and inconvenient cross-country journeys could be. Believe it or not I was not the prime-mover in those day-long odysseys of ours from Barrow-in-Furness to Bridlington. As a girl my mother had enjoyed holidays there, with her own parents, and once the war was over and my father, as a bank manager, could take the month's holiday to which he was entitled she was anxious to visit her old haunts. But the journeys, particularly the return, were positive marathons. There was no question of travelling light. We took an enormous cabin trunk, as well as many small pieces, but in those days porters were plentiful. The return journey was grand for railway sightseeing. The local from Bridlington took us no further than Selby, where we had to wait for a Hull-Leeds semi-fast. The lengthy wait, which the rest of the family did not appreciate, was pure joy to me. Two up East Coast trains, hauled by Great Northern Atlantics stopped at the platform on which we were waiting, and on the down through line there passed, in succession, the 9.50am relief, and then the 'Flying Scotsman' itself, both of course hauled by superheated Great Northern Atlantics.

The train from Hull, which we eventually boarded was hauled by an F class 4-4-0, and at Leeds, we transferred from the 'City' to the Wellington station to try our fortunes on the Midland. On the outward journey we had enjoyed the luxury of a through carriage from Barrow to Leeds, but no such facility was available on the return. We had to wait for the midday Edinburgh express from St Pancras on which a superheated Class 2 4-4-0 worked us smartly, and non-stop to Hellifield, and then another change, to an all-stations local to Carnforth. Finally, after a sight of West Coast expresses dashing through, there was the Furness 'parliamentary', to our own Furness Abbey. Why we spent so long in Leeds I cannot precisely recall, except that I have recollections that on one of our trips there was a scare of rabies, and all dogs had to be muzzled. Unprepared for this my mother and sister had to go out into the city and buy one for the family Pekinese, which looked indescribably comic balancing a totally unsuitable affair on the end of his pug-nose!

So far as journey times were concerned I looked up Bradshaw for the end of this particular period, and found that even though there was a through train from Leeds to Barrow in 1938-9, the total time from Bridlington was still 6hr 51min, and involved two changes. With the amount of luggage we had with us such changes of train sometimes produced 'panic stations', and losses of luggage were frequent experiences of travellers. Fortunately such a misfortune did not come our way, though one incident, hilarious to me in retrospect, was traumatic for my parents at the time. Arriving at the station for the homeward journey from one holiday my father suddenly found he was minus our return tickets. They were in a suit packed at the very bottom of that huge cabin trunk! With only 10 minutes to go before train time he wanted to unpack the trunk, there and then, in the middle of the station concourse. My mother strongly resisted, but got her way only by providing money for new tickets out of the remains of the housekeeping. Fortunately fares were relatively cheap in those days. Amid all the chaos I can't remember the class of engine that hauled us out of Whitby that day!

Below left: Furness Railway: a down stopping train in Furness Abbey station, hauled by 0-6-2T No 105.

Top: Another Box-Brownie shot on the Furness, showing a northbound stopping train in Sowerby Woods between Barrow and Park South Junction, hauled by a 6ft Pettigrew 4-4-0 No 130.

Above: Just after the Grouping of 1923: a Barrow to Carnforth stopping train between Furness Abbey and Dalton, hauled by 4-6-4T No 11102 newly painted in Midland red.

Below: London and North Western Railway, in 1921; a heavy up excursion train near Colwyn Bay, hauled by non-superheated 'Precursor' class 4-4-0 No 2115 *Servia*.

Top: LNWR Liverpool-Glasgow express near Hay Fell box, on the Grayrigg bank, hauled by 'Claughton' class 4-6-0 No 2101.

Above: LNWR: 4-6-2T No 1366 at Tebay; used for banking on Shap. This photo was taken in 1923 (note the coal wagon lettered LMS) but the majority of ex-LNWR engines were then still in the old colours.

Top right: LNWR Edinburgh and Aberdeen sections of the 10am ex-Euston on Tebay troughs, hauled by engine No 2222 *Sir Gilbert Claughton.*

Above right: The morning Liverpool and Manchester Scottish express on Tebay troughs, hauled by 2-4-0 No 1518 *Countess* and 4-6-0 No 110 *Lady Godiva* ('Claughton' class).

Right: One of the famous Aspinall Atlantics of the Lancashire and Yorkshire Railway in Liverpool Exchange station. The engine, No 10307, was originally No 1398 built in 1899.

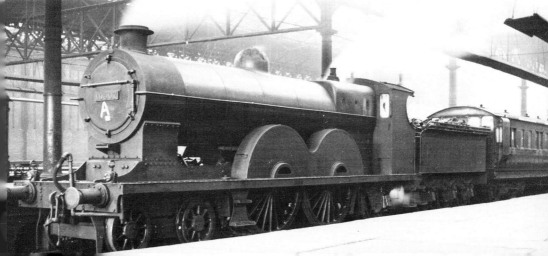

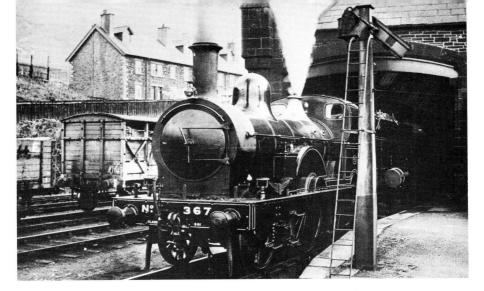

Top left: A Hughes 4-cylinder 4-6-0 of the LYR, rebuilt and superheated, leaving Carnforth with an up semi-fast train. Appropriately the leading coaches are LYR stock.

Above left: North Eastern Railway: a Box-Brownie shot of a Scarborough-Hull stopping train leaving Bridlington in 1920, hauled by an F class 4-4-0 No 1542.

Left: A lucky capture at Whitby in 1922. NER 1001 class 0-6-0 No 1275 (ex-Stockton and Darlington Railway and built in 1874). This engine has since been restored to its original condition and is in the care of the North Road Museum, Darlington.

Top: NER Fletcher 2-4-0 of the celebrated 901 class as rebuilt with Worsdell boiler mountings, on a Darlington train at Tebay, in 1923.

Above: NER Scarborough-Saltburn train leaving Whitby West Cliff, in 1922, hauled by 3-cylinder 4-4-4T No 2148.

2
The Southern
Constituents 1921-5

When I went to London in the autumn of 1921 to begin my engineering studies at the City and Guilds College, South Kensington, the railways running south of the Thames were my very first interest, and very soon I went to Victoria to watch the trains. Cameras were suspect on railway stations in those days and I was soon hauled up before the stationmaster, a portentious character, the breadth of whose waistcoat and gold chain, and his tailed coat was as impressive as the shine of his silk hat. But when he had accompanied me personally to the end of one of the platforms, and satisfied himself that I was not going to get tied up with the overhead electric wires, or jump on to the track all was well. Nevertheless I was warned that I really ought to have a permit.

The Brighton and the South Eastern and Chatham companies gave me lineside walking permits readily enough, and in succeeding years I enjoyed many happy days beside the line, between Purley and the north end of Quarry Tunnel, and between Elmstead Woods and Orpington; but a request to the London and South Western for similar facilities brought a peremptory 'No'! Permits on the LSWR were granted (or usually not granted!) by the Chief Engineer, and at this distance in time an experience of my great friend and fellow student Macgregor Pearson is good for a laugh. At one time, he was Hon Secretary of the college engineering society, and as such had to make arrangements for lectures, papers, and technical visits. He wrote to the LSWR asking for a party to visit the then-new hump marshalling yard at Feltham, and a few days later came storming into the theatre before the first college lecture of the day bursting with indignation: 'I've been insulted, by a man with a German name!'

The great A. W. Szlumper was then Chief Engineer of the LSWR and he had signed personally a particularly complete 'brush-off', saying such a visit could not possibly be allowed, because 'it meant going on to the track, which was *dangerous*'. Then he threw in a final 'stinger' saying that the application should have come from the principal of the college, and not a mere student (!). Recalling the many visits we made elsewhere, arranged entirely by the student-officers of various technical societies, Szlumper stood very much alone. For my own part I found useful vantage points from which to photograph LSWR trains near Clapham Junction and at Wimbledon, but my happiest hunting grounds were found during holiday visits to an uncle who then lived at Bournemouth. Shades of Szlumper! I wonder what he would have said if he had seen me squirming my way *underneath* his wooden pallisades to reach a highly photogenic lineside in Talbot Woods, west of Bournemouth Central station. I was slimmer then than I have since become!

Photographic permits aside, the Brighton was a fascinating line to the onlooker in 1920-1. I spent part of the school holidays at Eastbourne in the former year, and although to my disappointment there was a dearth of big engines, of the smaller there was a grand variety. My Box-Brownie snaps include I2 4-4-2Ts, 0-4-4Ts and 0-6-2Ts on the locals, while there were 'Gladstones' and 4-4-0s on the longer distance trains. On the London expresses there was an occasional Atlantic but more usually the B4 'Scotchmen' 4-4-0s were on the job. But the turnout of all engines was a delight. The Brighton was one of that choice band of English railways that had maintained its prewar engine livery through the dark days of 1914-8 and although Marsh's chocolate brown was a good deal less glamorous than Stroudley's yellow the deep rich colour was handsomely set off by the black and yellow lining and by the scarlet buffer beams, which were usually spotless. The carriages, all non-corridor even on the express trains, were then in matching brown.

The carriage interiors intrigued me. In earlier years I had grown accustomed to the attractive coloured views of scenes in the towns and country served by the Great Western. The London and North Western did the same, though in monochrome, while the Furness took every space above the seats to display the glories of the Lake District, with attractive maps to show where everything was. As for the Midland, the coach interiors and their pictorial displays were a model of good taste and elegant *décor*. Imagine then the shock of entering the carriage of an Eastbourne express on the Brighton line and seeing above the opposite seat a garishly coloured advertisement with the words: 'When Knights were bold they all wore armour; Nights hot or cold wear Swan's pyjama'. There were many other adverts in Brighton carriages, from which the company no doubt derived some badly needed revenue; but to a teenager brought up on the larger railways it seemed a bit crude.

In the autumn of 1921, when I did my first photography on the main line south of Purley, the Brighton had not added a single new express passenger engine to its stock since the two Baltic tanks of 1914. The motive power situation was thus entirely prewar in its vintage. In the spring of 1922 however a batch of five new Baltic tanks was turned out from Brighton works, the first and last of which were named, No 329 *Stephenson* and No 333, which became the war memorial engine *Remembrance* and was painted grey, instead of the standard brown. Until these engines took the road the two original Baltics *Charles C. Macrae* and No 328 had eluded me, when I was out with my camera, and equally so the two beautiful 4-6-2Ts *Abergavenny* and *Bessborough* remained quite occult, so far as I was concerned. The 'Southern Belle', in its first postwar form, had usually been hauled by Atlantics, while the B4 'Scotchmen', and the celebrated I3 superheated 4-4-2Ts shared many of the lesser trains. At that time the 'Belle', as a spectacle, was disappointing, because in addition to the Pullman cars it carried a short rake of ordinary flat roofed non-corridor carriages to provide third-class accommodation; and as these were marshalled next to the engine on the down morning train it made an undistinguished picture.

The introduction of the new Baltic tanks in 1922 brought a considerable change to the locomotive workings, and with the stud of these large engines increased to seven it was possible to cover most of the 60min expresses between Victoria and Brighton, as well as the famous 'City Limited', the stockbrokers express, to and from London Bridge. At that time most of the 4-6-4Ts were doing the return trip from Brighton to London twice a day, with the London Bridge turns linked in with those to Victoria by light engine running over the South London line when necessary. Thus the engine of the up stockbrokers express, 8.45am from Brighton, on arrival at London Bridge went light round to Victoria in time to work the down 'Southern Belle'. In days out on the line at Purley and Coulsdon I often photographed the same 4-6-4T twice in one day, both times on down expresses. By that time third-class Pullmans were coming in to use, but patrons of the 'Southern Belle' were evidently carrying more luggage than in prewar years, because it was found necessary to run a high-elliptical roofed bogie brake van next to the engine, again rather spoiling the gracious uniformity of stock that had once so characterised the 'Southern Belle'. A curious point, so far as my own observations went, was that with the coming of additional 4-6-4Ts the celebrated I3 4-4-2Ts virtually disappeared from main line work.

Soon after I went to London in 1921 I had the good fortune to meet the doyen of railway photographers, F. E. Mackay. I was invited to his home in Battersea, and he was such a kindly man that I, a mere stripling and beginner in the art of moving train photography, was welcomed as a fellow enthusiast. He had a particular interest in the Brighton line, and had a valued contact in T. B. Welch, then in the locomotive department at Brighton Works. Even with the introduction of the Nos 329-333 batch of Baltic tanks there was still a glorious uncertainty in the daily locomotive workings, but through Mackay and T. B. Welch I sometimes got a tip-off of something unusual for the forthcoming Saturday. That of course was the only day on which I could go down to Purley, or beyond. I may add that my goings and comings from South Kensington, where I was living, were entirely by push-bike. Our interest became centred upon the workings of two B4 class 4-4-0s which L. B. Billinton had recently rebuilt with larger boilers and super-heaters. From time to time I would get a note from Welch that No 55 would be on such and such a train, on the next Saturday.

These two engines were the final addition, or amendment to the express locomotive stock of the LB&SCR before the Grouping took place in January 1923. They proved excellent engines, and worked turn and turn about with the Atlantics and the big tank engines, on all duties up to, but not including the 'Southern Belle'. In January 1923 the top line motive power of the Brighton was thus:

(a)   Five non-superheater 4-4-2s, Nos 37-41
(b)   Six superheater 4-4-2s, Nos 421-426
(c)   Two 4-6-2 express tanks, Nos 325-6
(d)   Seven 4-6-4 express tanks Nos 327-333
(e)   Two rebuilt B4 4-4-0s, Nos 55 and 60

These were backed up by the 31 B class 4-4-0s the 'Scotchmen', and the 21 superheated 4-4-2Ts of Class I3. It was not a very numerous collection of engines, but they were all maintained in the superb state of mechanical efficiency traditionally bequeathed upon Brighton Works by Stroudley.

The South Eastern and Chatham, as I renewed acquaintance with it in 1921, interested me immensely. First of all there was the very striking change in locomotive painting style from what I remembered from prewar years. R. E. L. Maunsell was nothing if not a realist, and one of his first acts on coming to Ashford in 1913 had been to simplify the very elaborate engine livery adopted by the Managing Committee from 1899. With its wealth of colour in lining and underframe, not to mention the profusion of polished brass and copper work it was the most decorative of any in Great Britain, and that, in 1900-1914 also meant in the whole world. Maunsell suppressed everything except the basic green set off by a simple black and yellow lining; but as war conditions intensified he adopted the most austere finish that had yet been seen on a British locomotive — and all-over dark grey, without any lining, and the number carried in white sans-serif numerals on the tender. The tradition of smart finish on SE&CR locomotives prevailed however, and despite their excessively plain appearance they were kept very clean.

It was however not so much engine finish as the workings of several new types that attracted me to the SE&CR. The handsome new L class 4-4-0s, introduced just before the war naturally did not come down the Reading branch, and I had not seen one of them before our family moved up to Barrow-in-Furness in 1916. Then there were Maunsell's celebrated rebuilds of the D and E class 4-4-0s and lastly the prototype 2-6-0, No 810, and the 2-6-4T No 790. The rebuilt D and E class 4-4-0s had the Continental boat trains to themselves, and also some of the so called 'Kent Coast' trains. This latter name was applied to the services along the North Kent coast, to Margate and Ramsgate, over the former Chatham route. It is curious that Maunsell with his strong precepts of standardisation should have produced, in the fine L class 4-4-0, an engine that had only a limited route availability — all the more so in that the detail design, largely complete before Maunsell's arrival from Inchicore, had been done by Robert Surtees, a former Chatham man. But the L class could not be run over any of the former Chatham lines. It was the postwar decision to concentrate all the Continental boat train workings at Victoria instead of Charing Cross that produced an urgent need for engines of greater capacity than the non-superheater D and E class of the Wainwright era.

There was some beautiful weather in the late Spring of 1922, and I spent some happy Saturdays out on the line between Elmstead Woods and Orpington. I rejoiced not only in the trains themselves, which were not all that many, but in the glorious flowering trees in the country alongside. In the bleak countryside of Furness, and in the Craven country of the West Riding of Yorkshire one did not see the profusion of chestnuts, with flowers of all hues, nor of the lilacs, laburnums, and richly red hawthorn that distinguished many of the gardens that backed on to the railway. That however is a digression. On the Folkestone-Dover-Deal trains, and equally those to Hastings, one could be fairly sure of 'copping' an L class. They always seemed to be very much on top of the job, though the late Harold Holcroft, in his many letters and in the private conversations he had with me never seemed to have much of an opinion of them. Maunsell himself, who was more of a production man than a specialist engine designer, was sceptical of the valve setting prepared for them by Surtees and sent the details over to his former chief draughtsman in Inchicore, W. Joynt, for a check-up. But I always found them willing, hard working and free-running engines. Despite their drab colouring they were also highly photogenic, to a black and white camera.

One of the attractions of the South Eastern and Chatham was that the full boat train service operated on Sundays, and a cycle ride out to Bickley or Orpington gave the certainty of catching an E1 on each of the down expresses. The up workings always had their uncertainties because of the then-frequent late arrivals of the connecting trains at the French and Belgian ports. Continental railways were not then the models of punctuality that they subsequently became, and many were the tales of rough riding, late running, and of the hazards of travelling in such wooden coaches as were often to be found on fast trains in those first postwar years.

The South Western was a fascinating line to watch, from the touch-line as it were. My prime objects of interest were of course the new Urie 736 class 4-6-0s, the forerunners of the 'King Arthurs'. When I first went to London in 1921 there were only 10 of them. Most of them were stationed at Nine Elms, and one could be sure of seeing one on the 11am West of England express, which it worked to Salisbury. One of them sometimes took the 9.30am, semi-fast to Bournemouth, a heavy, but not a sharply timed train; but its interest for me was that the engine worked back at mid-afternoon and was ideal for photography up at Hinton Admiral. When staying with my uncle, whose home was not far from Bournemouth Central station I would often go out before lunch to see what came down on the 9.30am and then pedal out to Hinton Admiral in the afternoon to snap the return working. Sometimes the engine was one of the original Urie H15 class of 1913. There was usually a 736 on the 6.40pm up $2\frac{1}{4}$ hour train to Waterloo, but other than that all the faster Weymouth expresses were worked by Bournemouth engines and men, exclusively of the L12 or D15 classes.

The D15 class, Nos 463-472, as superheated by Urie, were lovely engines, as reliable in their performance as they were handsome to see. Some of my very earliest detailed logs were taken behind them, though I must admit I also had some very good runs with the L12, or 415 class. This was a class whose appearance was not improved by fitting of extended smokeboxes, and removal of the smokebox 'wings'. But their performance was revolutionised. The general opinion among South Western enginemen was that in their original and most handsome condition they were little better than the celebrated T9 Greyhounds. A particular memory of an L12, No 418, not one of the best, is of a journey on the first part of the 6.30pm ex-Waterloo on the Friday before Whitsun, in 1925. The train was heavy, but not excessively so, but on those Bank Holiday occasions the working times were considerably expanded, (without telling the passengers!), so that 104min, instead of 92 was allowed for the 79.3 miles from Waterloo to Southampton. Engine No 418 was being worked by an elderly, and distinguished looking driver who evidently took every advantage of the extra time allowed to him — very much so, because with signal checks and a stop from someone pulling the communication cord he managed to take 116min to reach Southampton. During the station stop, when water was being taken, I went up to the engine to see if anything was wrong. I told the cheery fireman I was taking a stop-watch record, but this proved no instigation to more enterprising running, and the last 28.3miles from Southampton to Bournemouth took 39min.

The faster Bournemouth trains were then composed mainly of corridor stock, though there was no hesitation in adding old non-corridor vehicles when strengthening was required at holiday times. A common formation was four of the older LSWR corridors forming the Weymouth portion of the trains, and one of the new 5-coach 'tea-car' sets detached at Bournemouth Central and working round to Bournemouth West. These so-called 'tea-car' sets were not used on trains like the 6.30pm down from Waterloo, or the 6.40pm up from Bournemouth Central which provided full dining facilities. One hardly ever saw a goods train on the LSWR during daylight hours, and with permission to visit Feltham so summarily refused those of us who were interested had no sight of Urie's big 4-6-2 and 4-8-0 tank engines, unless one of the former happened to be working a transfer goods across to Willesden, or Cricklewood. The South Western was also a considerably less colourful railway than I remember it in prewar days. Not only had the very distinctive two-tone carriage livery of dark brown with salmon-coloured upper panels, given place to an olive green to match the engines, but

Dugald Drummond's locomotive style, with a brown surround to the green on cabside panels and tenders, had been simplified to the olive green with black and white linings. But the turnout, as on most British locomotives of the period, remained immaculate.

Top: London, Brighton & South Coast Railway: a down express at Clapham Junction, hauled by one of the celebrated 'Scotchman' B4 class 4-4-0s built by R. J. Billinton; No 48 was one of the batch built in 1902 by Sharp Stewart & Co in Glasgow.

Above: One of L. Billinton's 2-6-0 express goods engines, No 340, built in 1914, at Battersea sheds.

Above: A vintage parade inside the roundhouse at Battersea. The engines, left to right, are No 34, non-superheated Class I4 4-4-2T; an unidentified I1 4-4-2, showing the very small and ineffective boiler, and two Billinton 'radial' 0-6-2Ts, the left hand one fitted with a Marsh boiler.

Above centre left: Brighton 'Pullman' car express in Star Lane cutting south of Coulsdon, hauled by 4-6-4T No 329 *Stephenson*, when brand new in 1923, and having a small indicator shelter on the right hand running plate.

Below centre left: A stopping train of vintage non-corridor stock near Balham, hauled by the 4-6-2T engine No 326 *Bessborough*.

Below: London and South Western Railway: up Bournemouth express near New Milton, including the then-new 'tea-car' elliptical roofed stock. The locomotive is D15 super-heated 4-4-0 No 465.

Top: Adams 4-4-2T (as reboilered by Drummond) at Axminster for working the Lyme Regis branch.

Above: One of the celebrated Drummond M7 0-4-4Ts of the LSWR No 676, on a down local train at Haslemere.

Left: A Urie rebuild, with superheater, of a standard Drummond 0-6-0 goods engine, No 306, here seen working an up main line goods at Seaton Junction.

Below left: Ex-SECR Maunsell rebuilt and superheated 4-4-0 No 1019 working an up stopping train amid the picturesque 'white cliff' scenery of the Folkestone Warren.

29

Above: Ex-SECR, a Stirling 0-6-0T engine No 1336, built at Ashford in 1888, for shunting and branch line service in Kent. When photographed this engine was used on the heavily graded Folkestone Harbour branch.

Left: Ex-SECR, one of the handsome Wainwright Class D 4-4-0s, No 1738, original built in 1901 by Sharp Stewart and Co, here seen working a Hastings-Ashford stopping train, leaving Rye.

Below: Somerset and Dorset Joint Railway, 4-4-0 No 16 on a stopping train to Clifton Down at Bournemouth West: note the distinctive lamp headcode.

3
Great Western –
Six Years of Transition
1921-6

To the majority of railway enthusiasts, young and old alike, the prospect of the Grouping in 1923 spread a feeling of impending gloom. Even the late Cecil J. Allen, writing under one of his several pen-names and usually imbued with all the journalist's eagerness to witness and comment upon anything new, succumbed to the pessimistic mood, and in *The Railway Magazine* of October 1922 wrote:

'It is a somewhat melancholy reflection that this is probably the last occasion on which the data, tabulated and commented upon in the present article [British Express Trains in the summer of 1922] will appear in the form to which readers have by now become so well accustomed. Next year British railways, with all their distinctive features and their individuality of character — the subject of fervent partisanship among their admirers to an extent that has no parallel the world over — will have become absorbed, one and all, into four vast soulless corporations. Competition save in certain limited areas which form points of contact between groups — as compared with the widespread areas which now represent contact between individual companies — will have become as dead as the Dodo. One line alone will remain as a recognisable entity, and that is the Great Western — most distinctive, perhaps, of all British lines in its character for enterprise, and certainly the centre of the keenest partisanship of any'.

Before my family moved north in 1916 I had been a staunch Great Western enthusiast, and on coming to London in the autumn of 1921 I made an early visit to Paddington. The old 'A' platform, beyond the end of No 1, and open to the public, was a splendid vantage point for watching the trains; but although I was to some extent prepared for it, from many published photographs, I was disappointed by the sombre and often dingy appearance of many of the locomotives. They were then plain green, devoid of any lining and of the glittering adornment of polished brass and copper work that I remember from earlier days. I had been in some way prepared for this by a sight of the Great Western engine sheds at Chester when bound for a holiday at Llandudno earlier in the year, when the dull aspect of Moguls, 2-8-0s, and the occasional 4-4-0 outside with the plain green generally grubby made something of a contrast to the gleaming 'blackberry black' of an LNWR 'Prince of Wales' 4-6-0 bringing in the up day 'Irish Mail'. Paddington in October 1921 was the same. Even *Princess Mary* taking out the down 'Limited' looked dull, while many of the big express engines had tapered cast iron chimneys, instead of the massive erections that used to flaunt those imposing copper tops. So, at first, the Great Western got a minimum of the time I had available for train observing and note taking.

The acceleration of the 'Cornish Riviera Express' to its full prewar standard of speed in that same October, and Cecil J. Allen's stirring account of its running did something to revive my interest, but in the last pre-Grouping summer with no occasion to travel on the line I concentrated my attentions elsewhere. But then suddenly, and brilliantly the metamorphosis began. The October issue of *The Railway Magazine*, 1923, arrived before I left home for the autumn term at the City and Guilds, and brought with it not only a picture of *Caerphilly Castle*, but the glad tidings that the decorative finish of old was to be restored on all the express passenger 4-6-0s. The very first Saturday I was in London found me at Paddington, and I saw a glittering *Caldicot Castle* take out the down 'Limited', followed by *Pembroke Castle* on the 10.45am Gloucester and Cheltenham train. I well remember the enraptured comment of two young onlookers at the end of Platform 'A': 'Aren't they lovely!' And lovely they certainly were, the more so as they served to underline the unchanging atmosphere of the Great Western in a railway world that seemed everywhere else to be disappearing into the melting pot.

The winter of 1923-4 was the busiest yet of my young life: the third year at College, with Finals at the end of it, and the unceasing race to write up, in acceptably neat form, reports on the great variety of experimental work that we did during the day. But as the spring term progressed I seemed to be holding the job down, and after Easter an occasional Saturday out on the line would make a salutary breather. The Great Western gave me lineside walking permits both east and west of Reading, and a day of heavenly sunshine found me down at Twyford waiting for the down 'Limited'. I was lucky that day. It was a Laira turn on Saturdays and at that time all the original 10 'Castles' were stationed at Old Oak Common. But there must have been some change in the working because *Chepstow Castle* was on the job, followed by *Pembroke Castle* on the 10.45am. I saw two others of the class that day: *Cardiff Castle* on the 8.15am up from Plymouth, and *Carmarthen Castle* on the up 'Limited'. This, I found later, was something of a 'bag', because on one day when I was out a year later I did not see a single 'Castle'. In 1924 most of the engines I saw during that first session at Twyford were still in plain green though *King Henry* on the 11.15am two-hour Bristol express, and *Evening Star* on the 'Torbay Limited' were both regally clean.

The summer of 1924 was a milestone in my life. I fancy that my father must have anticipated my success in the Finals at college, because well in advance he arranged, by way of a celebration, to spend the family holiday at Penzance, travelling thence via London and the 'Cornish Riviera Express'. To one who was becoming more and more of a Great Western enthusiast this was a delicious prospect — but a horrible thought, suppose I did not pass! Those exams, were a double-barrelled affair: first the session-end at the City and Guilds itself, and then 10 days later the London University Degree. After some palpitating moments all was eventually well, and strangely enough the first advice I had was a telegram from some scholastic and co-Gilbert and Sullivan fans reading:

'Examiners have said it,
And it is greatly to his credit,
He becomes a BSc.'

So, in August, we set off for Penzance; but on the journey down from Barrow my new found enthusiasm for the Great Western received something of a jolt. On the up Aberdeen express to which our through carriages were attached at Preston I logged two of the finest runs that ever came my way while the North Western atmosphere remained undisturbed on the West Coast route — first with a 'Claughton' and then south of Crewe with a 'George the Fifth'.

Next day my chastening continued. Instead of the hoped-for 'Castle' the down 'Limited' had a dingy all-green 'Star', the *Queen Elizabeth*, and although the load was well below maximum, because only one slip portion, for Weymouth, was carried during the period of the summer service, we did not do too well, even from the start. With no greater hindrance than one moderate permanent way check, and load reduced by slipping from 430 to 350 tons at Westbury we were $4\frac{3}{4}$min down on passing Exeter, and with that load stopped for a bank engine at Newton Abbot. A Mogul coupled on ahead, but stopping to attach, and then to put it off again at Brent consumed a lot of time, and we were the best part of a quarter-hour late on arrival at Plymouth. The occasion was not cheered by the weather, which had become miserably wet and cold after Taunton. Through Cornwall we were worked by Moguls, one engine of the class relieving another at Truro. We were greatly heartened towards the end of the long journey however when there came a marvellous clearance to a cloudless evening. We did on the other hand have the doubtful pleasure of a loquacious, but not well-informed fellow passenger from Plymouth, whose prime assertion was that the china clay dumps in the St Austell district could be seen from the Scilly Isles!

With the same old bicycle that had taken me to Grayrigg, Coulsdon, Hadley Wood, and to the South Western lineside in the New Forest, and nearly a month of leisure I was able to see a good deal of Great Western working in west Cornwall. Moguls predominated to the virtual exclusion of every other type west of Truro. I was favoured with a walking permit, and in coming to explore the sheds at Ponsondane I discovered quite by chance the delightful exception to the Mogul omniscience. For there tucked away at the back of the shed was a 'Saint', No 2917 *Saint Bernard*. The running foreman was most friendly, and told me that an Exeter engine came down each day on the 'West of England Postal'; its crew lodged and then went back at 6pm on the corresponding up train. The engine, I was told, went right through to Paddington, via Bristol, with one Exeter crew relieving another in St David's station.

That piece of snooping into the innermost recesses of the shed was a piece of luck. In our family circle nursery tea at 5pm was something of a ritual, whether we were at home or in furnished apartments at the seaside, and with good holiday appetites the feast tended to be protracted. I might never have been aware of the treasure trove waiting to be photographed at the station each evening. As it was, to my mother's dismay, I used to jump up from the tea table about 5.30, seize my bicycle and pedal off to some previously chosen vantage point along the line. Engine No 2978 *Kirkland* was the most frequent visitor on this job, but other two-cylinder 4-6-0s were *Lady of Lynn*, *Lady of Shalott*, and *Clevedon Court*, in addition, of course, to the catalyst of my entire enterprise, *Saint Bernard*. *Lady of Shalott* had been repainted 'in glorious technicolour', as the old movie tag used to go, but the others were plain green. Twice only did I see four-cylinder engines on this job — *Queen Matilda* and *Princess Victoria*, both at that time plain green.

The morning procession out of Penzance was impressive. The up 'Limited', at 10am was followed at 10.10am by the Liverpool and Manchester, still, in 1924, of LNWR stock in the old, much cherished colours. Then at 10.30 there followed the Wolverhampton, and finally at 11am the second London, carrying the through North British carriage for Aberdeen. This through carriage however was something of a 'have'. An old school friend of mine came to spend a week with us, down at Penzance, and at my recommendation returned to his place of business at Sheffield, by this service. But the Aberdeen through carriage was transferred at Truro to another train, which had no restaurant car! I never discovered what this particular contretemps was, because in later years the Aberdeen coach was conveyed through to Westbury, worked to Swindon via Chippenham, and attached to another train that had a restaurant car through from Swindon to York. Reverting to west Cornwall, however, all these trains used to steam out of Penzance hauled by Moguls, to be followed by the 12 noon, a new train introduced in the autumn of 1924, connecting at Plymouth with the up afternoon mail to Bristol.

At that time the up 'Limited', like its westbound counterpart, changed engines at Truro, and on our homeward journey 2-6-0 No 6350 was replaced by *Lady of Shalott*. The load was the usual one of five 70-footers from Penzance, and one 70ft brake composite from St Ives attached at St Erth. The addition of the Falmouth coach at Truro brought the train up to a still-modest tonnage of 255 to be taken on a non-stop to Plymouth. The inclusion of a stop at Par, to attach a coach from Newquay, came in later years. From Plymouth I was again disappointed in not getting a 'Castle', but our fresh engine, No 4066 *Malvern Abbey* was in sparkling form. The final series of 'Star' class engines had been built new in 1921 with tapered cast iron chimneys and finished plain green; but by 1924 *Malvern Abbey* at any rate was gloriously turned out in the prewar style. With a relatively light load of eight coaches, only 315 tons gross, it should have been an easy job; but the heavy 1.25pm from Exeter was running somewhat behind time, and delayed us outside Exeter itself, and thence on every adverse section of line as far as Patney. By Savernake indeed we had lost $12\frac{1}{4}$min, on schedule. But that train ahead must have gone like the wind from there onwards, for we ourselves were able to run the last 70.1 miles to the stop at Paddington in $61\frac{3}{4}$in min and to arrive only 3min late. I then saw that the preceding train, with a load of more than 400 tons, had been hauled by No 4006 *Red Star*, as beautifully turned out as our own engine.

My father had decided that I should do a post-graduate course at the City and Guilds in Railway Engineering, and in the more leisured programme of that year I was able to scout round for possible employment in the following summer. Meanwhile my interest in the Great Western remained in top gear, enhanced by Cecil J. Allen's first accounts of 'Castle' performance. I am afraid I was definitely a partisan at the time of the famous 'Castle' *versus* Gresley Pacific interchange trials of 1925, though I saw very little of them personally. Still a student, and dependant upon a modest expense allowance from home, I could not afford to travel on any of the test trains, and my actual observations were confined to seeing LNER No 4474 take out the 'Limited' on her last down journey from Paddington, and having paid a visit to my future employers in York Road, Kings Cross, seeing *Pendennis Castle* arrive from the north. In the crowd milling around the engine at the head of No 1 platform, I heard one onlooker explaining that the presence of a Great Western engine was the result of Grouping(!), while another suggested to his inquisitive wife that perhaps the regular engine had failed.

Shortly after the exchange was over I had another day's photography in the Reading area, and believe it or not, did not see a single 'Castle' all day. The down 'Limited' with 14 on, and going magnificently was hauled by *Malvern Abbey*, the 8.15am up from Plymouth by *Bath Abbey*, and the up 'Limited' also had a 'Star'. The veteran photographer H. Gordon Tidey was also in Twyford cutting for part of the morning, and he was utterly disgusted at the absence of the new engines. I never ceased to be amazed at the huge loads taken by 'Saint' class engines on the South Wales trains. The 11.55am from Paddington, for example, with a load of about 450 tons had to make some hard running to keep out of the way of the 12 noon 'Torbay Limited' as far as Reading. At that time also Bristol (Bath Road) shed had no more powerful engines than 'Saints', and although the London expresses imposed no very severe tax upon them there were some heavy duties down into the West Country and over the west to north line via the Severn Tunnel. All these trains then changed engines at Bristol. So far as the Wolverhampton services were concerned the Midland would not allow anything larger than 4-4-0s over the line between Yate and Standish Junction, because of a completely mistaken view of the effects of locomotives upon the track. By the arrangement of their balancing the 4-4-0 'Counties' had a far more severe hammer blow at speed than the 4-cylinder 4-6-0 'Stars', or of the 'Castles' for that matter; but dead weight per axle was the only thing that counted with the ill-informed civil engineers of the Midland Division of the LMS.

Certainly 1925 was a vintage year for the Great Western. Apart from the success of the 'Castle' class locomotives in the interchange trials with the LNER the whole line seemed to be tuned up to concert pitch. Engines and coaching stock alike were immaculate; the courtesy of the service, and pride in the job on the part of the staff were evident everywhere, and it was only at the busiest holiday weekends that punctuality tended to suffer. For my last holiday before taking up my job as a graduate trainee with Westinghouse we went to Paignton, and in the height of the season things got pretty chaotic on the Kingswear branch. The 4-6-0 locomotives were not then allowed beyond Paignton, so that every train with Kingswear connections had to change engines. Furthermore, the extensive group of carriage sidings at Goodrington did not then exist. The branch became single track within sight of the Paignton platforms, and with many of the Saturdays only trains terminating at Paignton, and the empty stock having to be drawn back to Newton Abbot the congestion that occurred can be better imagined than described. The second part of the 'Torbay Limited' was scheduled to make its first stop at Paignton on Saturdays, but when another of my family was travelling down there had been three signal stops even before Exeter. Despite this the train was only 8min late passing through St David's station. After that they got into the queue, and ended up with a stand for more than 20min at the Paignton home signal to arrive eventually in 273min from Paddington, 49min late.

The second batch of 'Castles', numbered 4083-4092 was just getting into its stride by the time of the summer service that year. *Berkeley Castle* and *Builth Castle* went new to Laira shed. They were kept for the heavier trains, leaving the 'Limited' on its summer loading in both directions to 'Stars'. Newton Abbot shed as yet had no 'Castles', and until the full summer service began the 'Torbay Limited' stopping in each direction at Exeter, was a very heavy train for 'Stars' to handle. In 1925 the summer service did not begin until 13 July, and on the Friday previous to this when we travelled down to Paignton the load out of Paddington was one of no less than 13 70-footers. Unlike the 'Cornish Riviera Express' it carried no slip portions; the full train, 500 tons gross behind the tender, had to be taken through to Exeter. The driver of engine No 4042 *Prince Albert* would have been fully entitled to stop at Taunton for a pilot up to Whiteball, but he not only disdained any help; he had kept sectional time from Bedwyn to Exeter despite a permanent way check costing about $2\frac{1}{2}$min. Actually we were 10min late into Exeter, but that was due to a crippling signal stop at Hungerford.

It was a magnificent piece of running, but as if it were not enough I was treated to another, equally good, on the 5.8pm up from Newton Abbot a fortnight later. It was a Saturday that time, and there was much reaction from running of extra trains. We were stopped by signals in some odd places: for 6min, for example at Tiverton Junction, and again on leaving Taunton, on our nominally non-stop run to Paddington. We left with no fewer than 16 on, 514 tons tare, and again an unpiloted 'Star', No 4026 *King Richard*. This train detached a slip coach at Newbury, reducing the load there to 480 tons tare, 515 tons gross, but even with this intermediate relief it was an astonishing feat of weight haulage to pass Old Oak Common West Junction, 138.9 miles from the stop outside Taunton, in $147\frac{1}{4}$min. Whether we could have kept the schedule time of 152min, for the 142.9 miles from Taunton to Paddington without any checks I cannot say, but it would have been a very close thing, and my enthusiasm for the Great Western had by that time gone sky high. But still I had not managed to get a run with a 'Castle'.

I went back to Paignton to spend the August Bank Holiday weekend with my parents, and on the following Tuesday returned to London on the train that had previously done me so proud. That time we did have one of the new engines, No 4085 *Berkely Castle;* but with three coaches less than on that epic Saturday the work was inferior throughout, losing $3\frac{1}{4}$min net on schedule. It was not a good introduction; but the runs I had logged with 'Stars', and the many photographs of sparkling engines that I had secured on the south Devon line, and on the Kingswear branch, amply compensated for that one slight disappointment, and my first winter in engineering practice included many pleasurable recollections of a halcyon summer. There was no time for any railway expeditions at first, and after Christmas the clouds of industrial disturbance began to gather again, with the likelihood of another coal strike. I went up to Barrow for the Easter weekend, and then less than a month later came the disastrous General Strike.

Long before things had got back to normal afterwards my own affairs underwent a considerable change. The next stage in my training with Westinghouse included a spell in the works at Chippenham. When I went there, at the beginning of June, passenger train services were still very much restricted. Although the General Strike had lasted for little more than a week both sides in the mining dispute were obdurate, and there was little sign of normal supplies of coal being available. Until imports from the Continent could be organised the most rigid economies had to be practised on all the railways. One emergency service that I remember well was the late afternoon train from Paddington to Plymouth. The normal 3.30pm departure was a 3-hour Exeter non-stop, with slip coaches for Westbury and Taunton; but this was cancelled, and the 4.15pm down, via Bristol, was carrying the traffic of both trains. The latter normally slipped coaches at both Chippenham and Bridgwater, but these were omitted to save weight, and stops were made instead. Even so it was a fairly heavy train, frequently worked by the first of the 'Stars' to be rebuilt as a 'Castle', No 4016 *Knight of the Golden Fleece*. This engine, it will be recalled, was afterwards renamed *Somerset Light Infantry*.

The ordinary 'winter' service was largely restored in July, including the two-hour Bristol non-stops, both of which slipped coaches at Bath. When the former 4.15pm from Paddington was restored to its normal working leaving at 4.30 it had, what was to me, a curious engine roster. The London 4-6-0 came off at Swindon, and was replaced by a Bristol 'Saint', which used to tear through Chippenham in terrific style. I had another disappointing 'Castle' run on this service. Engine No 4097 *Kenilworth Castle*, with a load of 425 tons, lost time all the way to Didcot, ambling along at 58 to 62mph — 53.1 miles in $56\frac{3}{4}$min — and ending 2min late into Swindon on a schedule of 80min. There the 2-cylinder engine No 2923 *Saint George* came on, and livened things up thoroughly. Our slip coach was detached at Chippenham at 65mph. *Saint George* was on that job continuously for several weeks. The 6.30pm express from Paddington, also a Bristol 29xx turn, was then non-stop to Bath, slipping a coach at Chippenham. This service, as was also the mid-afternoon up, was a sore point with the Westinghouse management of that time. On the 6.30pm senior executives, or visitors to our works, confined to the slip coach, had no access to the dining car, while the mid-afternoon local was so timed in its arrival at Swindon as *not* to connect with the 'Cheltenham Flyer', then leaving at 3.45pm.

I remember the action of a colleague temporarily stationed at Chippenham, who, on the eve of the General Strike received a telegram instructing him to report in London as soon as possible. He had that telegram after lunch; took a *taxi* to Swindon, caught the 'Cheltenham Flyer' on its last pre-strike trip, and with another taxi reached Head Office, at York Road, Kings Cross, just before closing time at 5.30pm. The 'Cheltenham Flyer', then allowed 75min, for the 77.3 miles from Swindon to Paddington was of course a very easy train from the locomotive point of view. It was however many years before repeated remonstrances from the Westinghouse management secured an alteration in the timetable whereby the 'Flyer' could be caught by the connection from Chippenham, or that a stop by the 6.30pm down enabled passengers to dine on the way. An interesting point in connection with those slip coach workings at Chippenham is that they were taken forward immediately, attached to a steam rail motor car, calling at Corsham, Box and Bathampton. Those intermediate stations thus had an excellent through service from Paddington in the later afternoon.

While all the faster services from London were then worked by 4-6-0 engines, the 4-4-0 'Counties' were still much in evidence on intermediate trains. At least one express on the Bristol line was regularly worked by them. This was the 5.30am down from Paddington to Penzance, moderately heavy, but not very fast. It was one of those trains that the Great Western timed not to exceed a maximum of 60mph so that horseboxes or other four-wheelers could be attached if necessary. It used to arrive at Chippenham shortly after we had started work, at 7.30am, and from the then-open end of our electric shop I used to see the 'Counties' come rolling in, usually with a load of about 300 tons. I used it to travel to Bristol one Saturday morning and the driver of No 3803 *County Cork* was precision itself in not exceeding 60mph, even down through Box Tunnel. Beyond Bristol it was worked by 29xx class 4-6-0s to Plymouth. I had photographed it several times in the previous summer climbing the South Devon banks. The Bristol-Salisbury trains however did not even get 'Counties'. They had inside cylinder 4-4-0s either of the 'Bulldog' or 'Flower' classes.

My parents were on holiday at Paignton again that summer. I travelled thence via London, instead of direct through Bristol, in order to get some further runs on the crack West of England trains. At the time I could scarcely believe the changed standard of performance that I noted in the autumn of 1926. None but imported coal was then being used, and it seemed to take the sparkle out of Great Western engine performance. I went down on the first part of the 3.30pm loaded to 440 tons, with engine No 4085 *Berkeley Castle*. We began fairly well, but drifting down from Savernake without steam, and very leisurely running over the Langport cut-off line told its own tale. We passed Taunton only just on time, and with such a load as 440 tons there was no chance of keeping the sharp concluding timing of 31min, past to stop over the 30.8 miles from Taunton to Exeter. Even without the signal checks experienced at the finish we should have been at least $2\frac{1}{2}$ and probably 3min, late on arrival.

It was the same when returning a fortnight later on the 5.8pm up from Newton Abbot, though on slightly easier schedules, and a load of 395 tons No 4096 *Highclere Castle* had no time to be booked against engine. But the dashing brilliance of Great Western running was quite absent, and the colour of the fireman's face on arrival at Paddington — black, not red! — was enough. I may add that on these two West of England journeys of 1926 engine Nos 4085 and 4096 were both handled by drivers of the highest reputation. The weather was not good during that holiday down in Devon, and I did far less observation at the lineside than in the previous year. I noticed also that there was a good deal of late running, even at mid-week, and the majority of locomotives were not so clean as I had remembered them. It was very much a sign of the troubled times. After my return to London, for the next stage of my training, I was glad to transfer my railway interests elsewhere, for a time. The years 1921-6 had certainly been years of transition on the Great Western — both ways!

Above left: Great Western Railway in 1922: the 'Cornish Riviera Express' passing Old Oak Common, hauled by 4-6-0 locomotive No 4005 *Polar Star.*

Left: A maximum load coal train from South Wales drawing into Old Oak Common yards, hauled by one of the standard 2-8-0 mineral engines.

Top: The 10.05am Liverpool and Manchester express (with LNWR stock) leaving Penzance, hauled by 2-6-0 No 5308.

Above: Birkenhead express leaving Shrewsbury, hauled by 'City' class 4-4-0 No 3708 *Killarney.* This engine was originally named *Ophir;* but was renamed to haul the first 'day excursion' to Killarney, non-stop from Paddington to Fishguard, in 1907.

Top left: GWR 2-cylinder 4-6-0 No 2903 *Lady of Lyons* in war time plain green.

Above left: Plymouth express at Rattery summit, South Devon, in 1925. Note the dining car next to the engine and many clerestory roofed coaches in the train. The locomotive is 4-cylinder 4-6-0 No 4070 *Neath Abbey*.

Left: Branch line train leaving Kingswear, with two through coaches for Paddington in the rear. The locomotive is a small 2-6-2T No 4548.

Top: The 5.30am Paddington-Penzance express (via Bristol) climbing the Rattery incline, near Tigley signalbox, hauled by 2-6-2T No 3121 and 4-6-0 No 2922 *Saint Gabriel*.

Above: The 11am Paddington-Penzance express at Rattery summit. On this day, in 1925, 2-6-2T No 3121, double-headed both the 5.30 and 11am trains from Newton Abbot to Brent. The train engine in this picture is 4-cylinder 4-6-0 No 4024 *King James* ('Star' class).

Top: Another shot of the 5.30am from Paddington, climbing Dainton bank, with 2-6-2T No 3188 assisting 2-cylinder 4-6-0 No 2984 *Guy Mannering*.

Above: At Plymouth, North Road, in 1926: 4-6-0 No 4060 *Princess Eugenie* couples on to the down 'Cornish Riviera Express' for the westward run to Penzance.

4

'Metroland'

In its independent days the Metropolitan Railway ran a strong and attractive publicity campaign advertising the natural beauty and social advantages of living in the Home Counties of Middlesex, Herts and Bucks. Housing estates under the auspices of the railway were developed in what the company christened 'Metroland', and they were backed up by fast and attractive train services. As a boy I had remembered the Metropolitan only from travelling on the Inner Circle, and from the sight of an occasional electric locomotive at Bishops Road, Paddington. But my interest was quickened by the arrival of the December 1920 issue of *The Railway Magazine* which included a frontispiece of a new type of 4-4-4T engine, and a very handsome machine at that. Even so, when I went to London in the autumn of the following year the 'Met' was relatively small beer for a railway enthusiast bent on exploring the many main line railways that entered London, and it could have remained so but for the strong friendship that I formed with a fellow student at the City and Guilds, Macgregor Pearson to whom the Great Central, and with it the 'Met', were then the breath of life.

One Saturday morning early in 1922 I called at the Great Central offices at Marylebone to enquire about a walking permit, not on the line that was jointly owned with the Metropolitan but on the purely Great Central link from Neasden to Northolt Junction, over which I understood that the freights ran. After a few preliminary enquiries I was ushered into THE presence: W. Clow himself, the Superintendent of the Line, a mostly courtly old gentleman, who was kindness itself. A walking permit was arranged there and then. On the first fine Saturday in early March out I went to Wembley Hill. The only trouble was there were hardly any trains! Apart from the two down expresses, 10am ex-Marylebone to Bradford, and the 12.15 to Manchester there was nothing on the down line all morning, and only once when I was there, in lonely and unproductive vigils, did there pass an up freight. But Pearson showed me his own snapshots, mostly taken around Harrow, and including several of Metropolitan trains. There were many vantage points that made unnecessary any walking permits, and so I went further afield, into Metroland proper.

The new Metropolitan 4-4-4Ts interested me very much. Knowing that beyond Rickmansworth there were some stiff gradients to be climbed, and that with most of the residential trains rapid acceleration was needed between stops it had been something of a surprise that having purchased six-coupled tank engines in 1915 there should have been a reversion to the 4-4-4T type, moreover with smaller cylinders than on the 0-6-4Ts. The introduction of these latter engines, in 1915, created a good deal of interest in this locomotive world, signalised by the production by the Locomotive Publishing Co Ltd, a fine coloured postcard from a

43

painting by 'F. Moore'. These four engines were evidently intended to be the future top line standard passenger type, and they were all named. But while the first two were named respectively after the Chairman and General Manager of the company, something of a precedent was created by naming the third after the engineer responsible for their introduction — Charles Jones — the Electrical and Mechanical Engineer (designations in that order). Engine No 96 was, I believe, the first British Locomotive to be named after its designer, while the gentleman was still in office.

I have reason to believe they were not very successful in fast passenger service. While the 0-6-4T type is a natural development from the 0-4-4T, of which the Metropolitan had a very successful class, 0-6-4Ts generally have been addicted to rough and unsafe riding. Certainly those on the Midland and on the SE&CR were so affected, and the relegation of the Met quartet, despite their high sounding names, to goods traffic after no more than four years hints strongly at the same trouble. Certainly when Charles Jones had to provide more power for the trains serving Metroland in the postwar years he designed something quite different. Alongside J. G. Robinson's massive 4-6-2Ts that hauled the companion Great Central trains over the Joint Line they were of modest proportions. The comparative dimensions were:

Metroland Tank Engines

Railway Type	*Metropolitan* *4-4-4T*	*Great Central* *4-6-2T*
Cylinders dia (in)	19	20
stroke (in)	26	26
Coupled wheel	5-9	5-7
Boiler pressure (psi)	160	180
Nom tractive effort (lb)	18,400	23,740
Adhesion wt (tons)	39	54

The Metropolitan outer residential trains mostly consisted of six non-corridor coaches weighing fully loaded about 220 tons. These the 4-4-4T engines managed comfortably.

In 1922 the Extension Line, as it was then known, was electrified only as far as Harrow, and there all the longer distance trains had to change from electric to steam locomotives. There was possibly one exception, though I was not able to verify it. On Saturdays only there was one midday train from the City that was booked non-stop from Baker Street to Northwood; whether it was actually non-stop and steam hauled throughout I am not sure. The only time I actually saw it was north of Pinner, when it was going well at about 55mph hauled by a 4-4-4T. North of Harrow the line was double tracked only, and there were many overbridges from which excellent photographic viewpoints could be obtained. In contrast to the line through Wembley Hill to Northolt there was always plenty of activity, though no down Great Central express until the celebrated 3.20pm ex-Marylebone — always known by the men on the line as 'Marylebone Liz', why I never discovered. I cannot recall ever having seen any Metropolitan engine other than a 4-4-4T during that first summer of observation. I believe the 0-6-4Ts were used exclusively on goods trains, and the older 0-4-4Ts were confined to the northern branches.

The Great Central engines were an absolute joy to behold. Not only were they beautifully proportioned, but they were all so regally clean. There was a stopping train down in the mid-morning hauled by a Neasden 'Director', and the first of the up expresses always had a Leicester Atlantic — surely one of the most handsome locomotive classes that ever run the road. Leicester shed had no more recently built engines than the Atlantics, and two of them worked up to London each day, returning on the 5pm semi-fast, and the sharply timed 6.20pm which ran non-stop to Leicester via High Wycombe. With no more than a double track north of Harrow it would have been difficult to find a path for a fast non-stopping train amid the many suburban trains of both the Metropolitan and the Great Central at the time of the homegoing rush hour traffic on the Joint Line. The 6.20pm down, which was a through express to Bradford, was always taken by a Leicester Atlantic.

My interest in the Great Central can be said to date from 1912. Up to that time *The Railway Magazine* did not regularly come into our family circle, but for some reason my father brought home the June 1912 issue. Attracted by the imposing appearance of the large boilered Atlantics I was then by way of becoming a strong Great Northern 'fan', and I remember being keenly disappointed on opening the magazine that it seemed to be almost entirely devoted to a railway of which I, at the age of seven, had scarcely heard — the Great Central. It was in fact a special number in celebration of the forthcoming opening of Immingham Dock, by their Majesties King George V and Queen Mary. My disappointment did not last long. A magnificent collection of Mackay photographs of trains at speed, backed up by numerous official pictures of standard locomotives of all types quickened my interest, and a visit to the stationer's shop in Reading where they sold the 'F. Moore' coloured postcards showed me that Great Central engines were not only handsome to look at, but that they were also gorgeously coloured. As it turned out however, except for one brief glimpse another nine years were to pass before I actually set eyes on one of them.

That glimpse, in the late summer of 1920, was one of those pieces of luck that sometimes come the way of the railway photographer. The family, spending a month at Bridlington, decided upon a day's outing to Scarborough. We travelled thence in a stopping train, hauled by the usual F class 4-4-0, but on making our last stop, at Seamer Junction, where the main line from York was joined I noted that the spacious station might be a good place for photographs. After I had had my fill of the spa, and the sea front at Scarborough I obtained parental authority to go back to the station, and on a fine afternoon to go out to Seamer, and rejoin them there when the train for Bridlington arrived. In Scarborough station there was a return GCR excursion for Sheffield, Nottingham and Leicester, hauled by a Robinson Atlantic in all its glory. To my delight the stopping train our to Seamer went ahead of this excursion, and my little Box Brownie was able to 'cop' it, with the engine giving a splendid smoke effect.

To a photographer, in 1922-3, the 3.20pm down from Marylebone was the most interesting train of the day. It was a double home turn to and from Manchester, worked on alternate days by Neasden and Gorton sheds. As I recall it, Neasden then had no larger express engines than the 'Director' class 4-4-0s. All the big Robinson 4-6-0s were at Gorton. In the ordinary way 'Marylebone Liz' was not a heavy train. Its basic formation was one of five heavy elliptical coaches, including buffet restaurant car, for Manchester, and a through carriage for Halifax, detached at Penistone, about 230 tons gross, behind the tender. One could reserve a seat in the buffet car, and be served with anything from afternoon tea to a massive steak at any time one liked on the journey. Because my photographic trips were usually on Saturdays I saw many of the big engines on

constituent companies, and had a distinguished record of achievement, not only in locomotive design but in all the other ramifications of his office. Robinson however felt that he was too old, and that the job should go to a younger man who would be able to remain in office long enough to establish, sustain and continue the new policies that would undoubtedly be needed in the new organisation. So the post was given to H. N. Gresley, formerly of the Great Northern; but Great Central influence became strong in another direction. Responsibility for locomotive running was invested in separate departments in the Southern, North Eastern, and Scottish Areas, and in the Southern Area W. G. P. Maclure, formerly of the Great Central, was appointed to this new post.

The immediate result of this was a long term trial of Great Central locomotives on the Great Northern main line. While Gresley, as Chief Mechanical Engineer, was not directly responsible for locomotive running there is no doubt he had a high regard for Robinson and his locomotives. It was in any case largely as a result of Robinson's action in declining the post of CME, and recommending a younger man that Gresley got the job. The first trial of Great Central engines on the East Coast main line came in the autumn of 1923, when one of the 'Lord Faringdon' class 4-cylinder 4-6-0s worked on certain of the heavy London-Leeds expresses as between Kings Cross and Doncaster. From the viewpoint of nominal tractive effort they were much more powerful than the large boilered GNR Atlantics — 25,145lb against 17,340lb — but the latter, with their wide 31sq ft grates, were much freer in steaming, and this first experiment was short lived. F. E. Mackay secured a magnificent photograph of the GCR engine No 1166 *Earl Haig* pounding up through Hadley Woods with the heavy 4pm out of Kings Cross, but I have not seen any details of her running while on that work.

The introduction of the fast 'Pullman Limited' trains in the summer of 1923 gave a further opportunity for a trial of Great Central engines, because both the 'Lord Faringdon' class and the 'Directors' both had the reputation of being very fast runners on their own line. But in June 1924 the LNER introduced a second all-Pullman service from Kings Cross, to and from Sheffield taking the GNR route to Nottingham, via Grantham, and thence over the GCR line. The Harrogate train, booked non-stop between Kings Cross and Leeds, covered the 185.7 miles in 205min, at an average speed of 54.4mph, while the Sheffield Pullman covered the 128.7 miles to Nottingham at exactly the same average speed, taking 115min, to cover the 105.5 miles from Kings Cross to passing Grantham. I was out beside the line one morning in the summer of 1924, north of New Barnet, when *both* Pullman trains were hauled by Great Central engines. The 11.5am to Sheffield was hauled by the 2-cylinder 4-6-0 No 425 *City of Manchester* followed 10min later by the war memorial 4-cylinder 4-6-0 No 1165 *Valour*. I have never seen any logs of the running of the 'Sir Sam Fay' class on the former train, but the 'Faringdons' did much fast and adequate work on the Harrogate Pullman, being stationed at Leeds, Copley Hill shed for the purpose.

Although this is taking the story rather far away from Metroland I must add that the 4-cylinder 4-6-0s were eventually replaced on the Pullman trains by 'Director' class 4-4-0s, again working from Copley Hill shed. At one time the Harrogate train, extended from Newcastle to Edinburgh, had a non-stop run from Kings Cross to Harrogate in each direction, running via Spofforth and Church Fenton. The distance via this route was 198.8 miles, and schedule time 220min, involving an average speed of 54.2mph. The load was normally one of six Pullmans, amounting to about 255 tons behind the tender. So far as my own observations went the engines allocated to this duty were all of the 'Improved' variety of 'Directors' having 8in, piston valves and long travel. There was some fast running on occasions, but this of course was nothing new with Great Central engines.

Those of us who so admired the beautiful lines and elegant proportions of all the Robinson engines began to note a most unpleasant trait in their external appearance. Locomotives newly outshopped from Gorton had chimneys of Great Northern type, which soon became sarcastically nicknamed as 'flowerpots'. On 'Directors', 'Fays', 'Faringdons' and the Atlantics they looked a shortened version of the standard Doncaster type used on the large boilered Ivatt Atlantics. The transition, so far as Great Central engines were concerned, was a classic example of how to ruin the appearance of a locomotive. That chimney looked perfectly in keeping with the GN Atlantics, handsome, dignified ensemble; but substituted for the shapely chimneys of Robinson's engines it looked ghastly. It is hard to imagine why it was done. I know that chimneys became worn inside, by the abrasive action of the blast; but the 'Directors' that were so treated were only six or seven years old. I am afraid some of us who recoiled at the sight of those chimneys took the uncharitable view that someone at Gorton was seeking to curry favour, in a very crude way, by Great Northernising engines passing through for repairs. For the record, engines that I noted working on the Pullman trains, to and from Kings Cross, were *Butler-Henderson*, *Gerard Powys Dewhurst*, and *Marne*. When I began to use those trains, as from 1930, the 'Directors' had returned to their home ground, and the GNR Atlantics had the duties entirely to themselves.

There was an interesting interchange between Great Central and Great Northern engines in another respect, in that four of the 'Immingham' class mixed traffic 4-6-0s were moved from Sheffield to Copley Hill, and their places at Sheffield taken by four GN large boilered Atlantics. Between Doncaster and Leeds the London expresses had hitherto been worked by Moguls, usually of the 3-cylinder K3 type; but the 'Imminghams' which I first logged on those duties in 1928 put up some sparkling performance. They too suffered from the 'flowerpot' disease, and also from another insidious neo-Gortonism — squashed-flat dome covers, about the height of those seen on a Gresley Pacific. But oddly enough, they were one of the second-line LNER engine classes that continued to be painted green. Only a few favoured classes, other than the Pacifics survived the 'economy-black' campaign that submerged 'Directors', Atlantics, and all other GC express types, except the 'Faringdons'; but quaintly enough the 'Imminghams' escaped — at any rate for as long as I saw them.

I mentioned earlier that Gresley has a soft spot for the Great Central engines. When additional passenger engines were needed for the North British section in 1924 the 'Improved Director' type was chosen in preference to the indigenous 'Scott' class, even though the nominal tractive efforts were almost identical. Both had 20in by 26in cylinders, and the 180lb pressure of the GC engine, against 170, was balanced by 6ft 9in against 6ft 6in coupled wheels. The Great Central engines with their much larger fireboxes and grates had the greater potentialities, and they were, in my experience, much freer running engines. The choice was justified on that account. To suit the Scottish loading gauge the boiler mountings had to be cut down, and on these engines the truncated 'flowerpots' did not look too bad. But when Gresley authorised construction of a further batch of ex-GCR 4-6-2Ts (LNER Class A5) for use in the North Eastern Area the effect was horrible. The chimney was the full-sized 'flowerpot', and the dome cover was that of a Pacific!

Left: Harrow-on-the-Hill, 1922: Aylesbury train pulling out, after having changed its electric locomotive for one of the handsome Metropolitan 4-4-4Ts.

Below: Up Great Central stopping train just south of Harrow, hauled by 4-4-0 locomotive No 434 *Earl of Kerry* ('Director' class).

Bottom: Aylesbury train leaving Rickmansworth, hauled by Metropolitan 4-4-4T engine.

Top: At Sheffield Victoria, GCR 4-6-0 No 196, one of the two built with 6ft 9in coupled wheels for competitive running against the Atlantics.

Above: Great Central outer-suburban train near Chalfont Road, hauled by a Robinson 4-6-2T No 451. Note, the anti-collision serrations on the leading coach, just above the sole bar.

Right: At Rickmansworth, after electric traction had been extended thence: an Aylesbury train leaving, after having just changed from electric to steam traction.

Above: Down GCR stopping train near Pinner, hauled by 'Director' class 4-4-0 No 437 *Purdon Viccars*.

Left: GCR outer suburban train, composed of old style coaches leaving Rickmansworth, hauled by 4-6-2T locomotive No 454.

Top right: The Great Central spreading its wings: the short-lived 11.5am. Sheffield Pullman from Kings Cross passing through Hadley Woods hauled by GCR inside cylinder 4-6-0 No 425 *City of Manchester* ('Sir Sam Fay' class).

Above right: An ex-GCR 2-8-0 mineral engine on down GNR line goods in Hadley Woods.

Right: The ravages of Grouping! One of the once-beautiful GCR 1020 class 4-4-0s disfigured after Grouping by flowerpot chimney and flat dome cover: locomotive No 6040 (GCR No 1040) at York.

5
Great Eastern: Great Northern

When I went to London in October 1921 I was no stranger to the Great Eastern. As a pre-teenager I had travelled on it in its Royal Blue days, to Felixstowe. Then for a Christmas present in 1916 I was given a copy of the Rev J. R. Howden's beautiful book *Locomotives of the World*, illustrated throughout in colour with reproductions of the famous 'F. Moore' oil paintings. Furthermore these were not merely the pictures familiar on picture postcards issued by the Locomotive Publishing Company, but in every case new ones, commissioned specially for this book. It was not a new publication in 1916. The text was definitely 'dated', to around 1909. In the chatty essays that accompanied each of the beautiful coloured plates the reverend gentleman was no more than slightly technical; but one passage in his piece about the Great Eastern stuck in my mind, even at that early age. He wrote, of the 'Claud Hamilton' class 4-4-0s:

'The only objection which the most captious critic could bring against the appearance of these fine locomotives is that they are perhaps a little gaudy. Tastes differ, but I must confess that blue, red, white, yellow and black, to say nothing of polished brass, copper and steel-work, all crowded on to one engine, appears to me not only a little overpowering, but also needlessly extravagant. I should very much like to see one of our big lines adopt a kind of battleship grey for the groundwork of its engines, relieved, say, with white lines and lettering.'

Several of the British railways adopted a simplified style of painting for their locomotives during the war years. Several of the Furness 0-6-0 goods engines were painted battleship grey. But in the photographs reproduced from time to time in *The Railway Magazine* there was nothing to suggest that any austerity measures had been taken on the Great Eastern. It so happened however that the first railway journey I made out of London in October 1921 was to Bishop Stortford, to play rugger, and my surprise can well be imagined when I saw all the locomotives in and around Liverpool Street, suburban and main line alike, all in battleship grey! Was it indeed a coincidence that Howden's general suggestion had been taken up, as a wartime measure on the very line he had so gently criticised? I do know however that the directors of the Locomotive Publishing Company had a rather special association with the Great Eastern, and with Stratford Works in particular. They would have been more than usually interested in a book wherein the paintings of their own artist had been more finely reproduced than anywhere else before or since, and the author's comment about the lavishness of the original engine livery may not have passed unheeded.

My own associations with the Great Eastern in my early years in London, were threefold. I was of course eager to photograph the main line express trains out in the country, but to us budding engineers the Great Eastern had a special attraction in that its main locomotive works was just on the outskirts. Apart from Stratford, the nearest main works was more than 50 miles away, at Brighton. The management at Stratford had no inhibitions about young engineering students making a conducted tour of the works, and thence we went, one memorable Saturday morning. Their readiness to welcome us may have been in part due to the Dean of the City and Guilds College, the very eminent Professor W. E. Dalby, having spent part of his earlier career in the locomotive department of the GER. That however is by the way. But the third facet of my early interest in the Great Eastern was centred upon the suburban workings. It was in 1915 during the dynamic general managership of Henry W. Thornton, that an unprecedented staff appointment was made. F. V. Russell, Chief Draughtsman in the locomotive department, was taken away from what would otherwise have been his lifetime's work in mechanical engineering, with the likelihood of eventually becoming Chief Mechanical Engineer, and appointed Superintendent of Operation. Very soon after his arrival from the USA, Thornton had begun a drastic reorganisation of the main line services of the Great Eastern; but the London suburban was a far greater task, and Russell will always be remembered for the outstanding metamorphosis he was eventually able to carry out. I personally shall remember him in another way, but more of that anon.

First however, so far as lineside photography was concerned, the Great Eastern was the one line running out of London to which I did not journey on my old bicycle. The thought of riding through the City, and then continuing through the crowded purlieus of the East End was rather too intimidating, and at first I used a bus that ran through from Victoria to Seven Kings and Chadwell Heath. But the scenery there was not very attractive, and on later expeditions, armed with a walking permit, I spent some long happy days at the lineside in the deep cutting between Brentwood and Shenfield. It was an ideal place for one with as modest an apparatus as my own. The summit of the Brentwood bank was in that cutting, and with graceful bridges and tree-lined slopes there were many picturesque locations. The line was then no more than double tracked, and the speeds of even the fast express trains were rarely more than about 30mph. The fact that there was a long curve was also fortuitous, because as the afternoon sun moved round I could move my position from Brentwood to the Shenfield end of the stretch, and photograph the early evening up expresses from the down side. Generally speaking 4-6-0s were on the heaviest trains such as the 12.30pm to Yarmouth and Lowestoft, and the 3.10pm to Cromer, but a surprising number of the long distance expresses were hauled by the 'Claud Hamilton' class 4-4-0s, all of which, at that time, were still non-superheated.

The normal formation of the regular express trains always consisted of the latest elliptical-roofed bogie corridor coaches, but there seemed precious few of these to spare. At holiday weekends, when there was an extra rush of passengers, and the normal formations had to be strengthened the extra coaches added were often non-corridor six-wheelers. In these days of fixed formation train sets, such as the British Railways HST sets it would seem incredible for a train to be strengthened at the last minute. But it was not unusual at Liverpool Street for the traffic department to decide at the very last minute to add an extra coach, or coaches, even after the train engine had backed on and coupled up! Great Eastern loads in the holiday season matched those of the London and North Western, though not reaching the staggering proportions of those worked on the Great Western in the height of the summer.

Stratford Works had a great and proud tradition of locomotive design and construction. It was the first big works I had ever visited, though I had been prepared in some way for the general style of operation in the various shops by a walk round the Furness Railway Works at Barrow a few years earlier. When I went to Stratford the Great Eastern was busy augmenting its stud of superheated 4-6-0 locomotives, and had just taken delivery of a batch of 20 from Beardmore's, in Glasgow. This class, for the design of which F. V. Russell was largely responsible, was extremely successful. Although not large by contemporary standards, and by track restrictions limited to an adhesion weight of only 44 tons, they were capable of handling very heavy loads, up to 450 tons, on the sharp timings of the Hook of Holland boat express, and the principal Cromer and Yarmouth trains. I saw several of these engines in various states of repair in Stratford Works, and although I was not sufficiently experienced to appreciate the finer points of constructional practice I remember being very impressed with the sense of pride that all the men working on them displayed.

The running of the principal Great Eastern expresses at that time involved hard running up the numerous short gradients on the main line, in addition to the tremendous 'slog' up the Brentwood bank on the outward bound journeys. But there was no call for sustained fast running on the favourable stretches of line. Maximum speeds did not often exceed about 70mph. For this kind of duty the proportions of the 1500 class 4-6-0s were ideal: large cylinders, 20in diameter by 28in stroke; large diameter piston valves, 10in giving generous port openings, and a splendid boiler, and a grate area of 26.5sq ft. The very long and commodious cab made the engines look a great deal larger than they actually were. The boiler barrel was only a few inches longer than that of the Great Central 'Director' class 4-4-0, and with that long cab completely astride the rearmost pair of coupled wheels, there were long wooden benches inside, covering the wheel splashers. Inside, those cabs were not nearly so roomy as they might have appeared, and the fireman had to work in a channel between the two wooden benches. The rebuilt engines (LNER Class B12/3) were the same, and I found then uncomfortable engines to ride, sitting upon the left hand bench, with one's feet dangling in the direct line of the fire. The firedoor also, was an unusually long way from the shovelling plate of the tender, necessitating a step or two between each shovelful. It was on this account that the men of the GN of S nicknamed them the 'Hikers'.

Russell's reorganisation of the surburban workings, in and out of Liverpool Street, the Jazz service as it became known, was a masterpiece of time and motion study. The Great Eastern had no money to spend on grandiose schemes of modernisation — new signalling, track alterations, electrification and so on. It had to be done with existing tools. A. J. Hill's 0-6-2T engines, that became LNER Class N7 were very few on the ground, and the service was based, believe it or not (!) on the little 0-6-0Ts of James Holden's design, dating back to 1890. They had cylinders no larger than 16½in diameter by 22in stroke; the coupled wheels were 4ft 0in diameter, and the first batch of them that was built for passenger service, and equipped with the Westinghouse brake carried a boiler pressure of 140lb sq in. This was first increased to 160 and ultimately to 180lb sq in. Even so they were tiny little engines, though very handy for the job. I have always felt that historically they have never been awarded the honour they deserve. In his famous series of articles in *The Railway Magazine* Ahrons does not even mention them; yet those 109 engines (LNER Class J69) were doing a job that would make the Brighton 'Terriers' die of fright! In the rush hours — or what the Great Eastern more appropriately called them, the crush hours! — they were working trains of

16 4-wheelers, at a traffic density of 24 trains per hour on the busiest section — with mechanical signalling too.

The passengers were expected to fall in with the breathless 'time and motion study' *motif* of the whole service. When recently I had an opportunity of watching the commuter services around Chicago, and passengers entering the huge double-decker cars of the C&NW railroad, with unbelievably long station stops, I thought of Russell and his methods on the Great Eastern in 1920. The large figures, 1, 2 and 3, on the coach doors were not considered enough to segregate the three classes of passenger readily enough, and ensure they entered promptly. Doors of the first class were painted yellow, and those of the second class blue. It was this colouring that led to the service being nicknamed the 'Jazz'. Russell himself was invited to lecture to the Engineering Society at the City and Guilds College, and he gave a performance fully in keeping with the magnificent train service he had inaugurated. He was no orator. He read from a typed script at top speed, pausing occasionally to mop his brow, and to take a gulp of water, from the array of tumblers placed on the desk in front of him, as much to typify the servicing of the little 0-6-0T engines on which he depended so completely. As a locomotive engineer he would be well enough aware of their capacity, and of their limitations. That the 'Jazz' worked like well-oiled clockwork was a tribute to the realism with which he had planned it. I recall equally that we students were too overcome with the volume of statistical and engineering data that had been hurled across in so short a time that there were hardly any questions!

It seems extraordinary on recalling it that when I first went to watch the trains at Kings Cross, and by the lineside at New Barnet that there was no train known officially as *The Flying Scotsman*. The name, whether 'Scotsman' or 'Scotchman' was used frequently enough by non-professionals who nattered about railways; but among this loosely linked fraternity there seemed a strange uncertainty about which train, and indeed which *railway* could claim the title. I have in my collection a coloured picture postcard issued by Raphael Tuck entitled *The Flying Scotsman*. What is actually depicted, very pleasantly and accurately, is an up West Coast sleeping car express hauled by an 'Experiment' class 4-6-0 of the LNWR on Bushey troughs! *The Railway Magazine* of 1922 commenting editorially on the summer train services of that year simply referred to the '10am express', while in the same volume captions to photographs '10am Anglo-Scottish Express' were applied equally to trains departing from Kings Cross and Euston. The great event of 1922, of course, was the introduction of the first two Gresley Pacifics, Nos 1470 and 1471. Not all the 'fans' were pleased. I remember one fellow student who had a mild interest in railways refer to them as 'useless, expensive mammoths'; but F. E. Mackay, who was soon out photographing them remarked to me: 'It'll be a long time before we see them being piloted!' This arose from the fact that in cases of very heavy loading the Atlantics were piloted from Kings Cross out to Potters Bar.

Train working over the Great Northern main line, over which the mineral traffic was quite heavy, was governed to a marked extent by the double-line bottlenecks through the tunnels from Greenwood Box to Potters Bar, and then over Welwyn viaduct through the two further tunnels to Woolmer Green. On the quadruple tracked sections north of the latter point permissive working was in force for the heavy freight trains, and they used to queue up, nose to tail. To provide the necessary gaps for some, at any rate, of these freights to get through without too much delay the passenger trains were grouped in 'flights' like the HSTs on the Western Region today. Northbound from Kings Cross one had the

10am and 10.10 departures, preceded at busy times by the 9.50am relief to the 'Flying Scotsman'; then, in the early afternoon came the 1.15, 1.30 and 1.40pm expresses, and finally the 5.30 and 5.40pm. There was, intermediately, the very heavy 4pm down express, which seemed to have a through carriage for everywhere on the line, while in 1923 the long forenoon gap between the 10 o'clock and the 1'o'clock flights was broken by introduction of the all-Pullman trains. In the up direction the first major group of expresses came into Kings Cross between 1 and 2pm, and a somewhat wider separated 'flight' from 5pm onwards.

When I first went out photographing, all these train would, without exception, be hauled by the large boilered superheater Atlantics, and even on the heavy 4pm down I never saw one of them piloted. When the first two Pacifics came on the scene No 1470 *Great Northern* was kept at Doncaster. The riding was not all that it might be, and some adjustments and alterations had to be made to the suspension. The second engine, at first unnamed, was allocated to King's Cross, presumably for prestige purposes, and worked the 10am down to Grantham. At that time it was neither a fast nor a heavy train, but it gave the engineman the 'feel' of the new machine. On my return to London in 1922, after the long vacation. I went out to Oakleigh Park and positioned myself on the footbridge just south of the station; but although it was a beautifully fine morning there was one of those annoyances to train photographers — a strong cross-wind. No 1471 was steaming very lightly as she ambled uphill at about 40mph and the exhaust steam blew down and obscured everything beyond the leading coach in the train.

Although one could have some long waits for expresses when photographing at the lineside of the GNR there was plenty to see in between times. The heaviest mineral trains were usually worked by 2-8-0s. The latest 3-cylinder variety, later LNER Class 02 were coming into traffic, but there were plenty of the original 2-cylinder type, with their immensely long connecting rods. They were always travelling very slowly, and were easy prey for my modest camera. There was a great art in handling the lengthy mineral trains, often made up to 1,300 tons gross behind the tender. There were separate goods lines between New Barnet and Oakleigh Park to keep these slow trains clear of the slow-line platforms used by the local passenger trains. The old saying that 'every picture tells a story' had its point one day, when at Oakleigh Park I saw the 2-8-0 that had run through the catch points at the end of the up goods loop, and nosed into the soft ground of the cutting side beyond until its front was buried almost up to the funnel. The long train must have got mildly out of control and quietly pushed its engine into the ground!

The local trains were very interesting. Gresley's relatively new superheated 0-6-2Ts had a complete monopoly of the purely Great Northern services, from Kings Cross and Moorgate. Their non-superheated predecessors had entirely disappeared. From time to time I used to travel out to New Barnet to play rugger, and the working of the suburban trains by the superheated engines was always very snappy. Interspersed with them were those of the North London originating from Broad Street. These were quite fascinating, hauled by the little 4-4-0 outside cylinder tanks, in the LNWR colours. The trains were composed of close-coupled four-wheelers of somewhat antiquated design; but the timetabling in the peak periods involved some close-headway working, and those little veterans had to step it out in keeping with the Great Northern trains, and they made a remarkably good showing. Some of the North London trains terminated at New Barnet, while others continued to Potters Bar.

A new Great Northern class, which had greatly excited my imagination, was the 1000 class Mogul introduced in 1920. They had created much interest from the unusually large diameter of the boiler, namely 6ft, and the use of 3-cylinders. Later of course we realised that their design was a logical step in the development of Gresley's constructional policy. In Great Northern days there were only 10 of them, numbered 1000-1009; but they were painted in the passenger engine style, and must have looked superb. I never saw one of them myself, but a large folding colour plate in *The Railway Magazine* in 1920, gave, what I imagined was a very faithful impression of them. The 0-6-2 suburban tank engines were also painted green, but all the heavy freighters, and also the 2-cylinder Moguls of the classes that became LNER K1 and K2 were finished in battleship grey, with white lettering lined in black. The K1 series numbered 1630-1639 were not often seen near London. They had originally been painted green on their first introduction in 1912, as were the first batches of the larger K2s; but they were all in grey when I saw them from 1921 onwards.

The first occasion I had to travel in an express train on the Great Northern main line came in the early summer of 1923. I was to spend the first part of the long summer vacation with my old school friends at Leeds. By that time several of the first post-Grouping batch of Gresley Pacifics were at work, and I had learned that they were regularly on the 4pm and 5.40pm expresses down from Kings Cross. The former, in deference to its great weight, and to make it manageable by an Atlantic if a Pacific were not available, then had a very easy timing to Peterborough. It was not nearly so attractive a proposition from the speed recording viewpoint as the succeeding 5.40pm; but in deference to the convenience of my hosts in Leeds I thought it desirable to take the earlier, and slower train to avoid too late an arrival. It was a decision I have never ceased to regret.

At the time of its formation in January 1923 the LNER had Pacific engines of both Great Northern and North Eastern design; and while shortly afterwards Gresley was appointed as Chief Mechanical Engineer, Sir Vincent Raven of the North Eastern, who was far senior to him in years had been appointed consulting engineer to the new company. Before Grouping the Great Northern had placed an order on Doncaster Works for 10 more Gresley Pacifics, Nos 1472-1481, but while naturally Gresley would have a preference for his own design the situation was rather delicate; and before deciding on his future standard he arranged a series of comparative trials using the North Eastern dynamometer car. No news of these impending events reached the technical press, and I learned afterwards to my chagrin that the Raven Pacific No 2400 had worked the 5.40pm down from Kings Cross to Doncaster on the very day I had travelled down on the 4pm.

While other than this brief encounter there was a distinct sameness about the engine workings into Kings Cross in those first years of the Grouping era I found that there was a great variety of locomotives usually to be seen on shed at Hitchin. In his first years as Locomotive Engineer of the GNR H. A. Ivatt had built a considerable variety of 4-4-0 engines. As things turned out few of them were used on the principal main line express workings and at the time of Grouping these were being used on all kinds of secondary jobs. Some of them had certainly come into their own briefly as main line pilots in the postwar years when assistance was given to the Atlantics between Kings Cross and Potters Bar in cases of exceptional loading. When the Pacifics were becoming well established, and schedules tightened up a little, 4-4-0s were sometimes used throughout Atlantic workings, when these latter had to be substituted in what were normally Pacific rosters. To indulge in double-heading at all had been little short of sacrilege of the Great Northern down from the days of Patrick Stirling, who made it impossible on his 8ft bogie single express engine by not carrying the vacuum pipe through to the front buffer beam! In LNER days the conscience of the running department had been more elastic, and I have details of a run up from Peterborough taken in February 1931 on the up Harrogate express due in Kings Cross at 5.10pm on which a load of no more than 415 tons was taken by Atlantic No 4461, leading, and 4-4-0 No 4331 next to the train. This latter was one of a batch built by H. A. Ivatt in 1898. Ironically, it was one of the poorest runs I had experienced on the Great Northern main line up to that date.

Left: Great Eastern Railway: Cromer express nearing the summit of the Brentwood bank, hauled by 4-6-0 No 1535.

Below left: Another typical pre-Grouping scene on the GER: Cromer express passing Gidea Park, with local trains in both loop line platforms, 4-6-0 No 1523 on the express.

Above: One of the two 'Super-Clauds' stationed at Kings Lynn for Royal Train workings to and from Sandringham: 4-4-0 No 8787, here seen at Kings Cross.

Below: Just after Grouping, with the engine painted in LNER green: up Yarmouth express at Ingrave summit, between Shenfield and Brentwood, hauled by 4-6-0 locomotive No 8552.

Top: Deployment of the ex-GER stud: one of the 4-6-0s at Kittybrewster sheds, Aberdeen, for use on the Great North of Scotland section.

Above: A Holden mixed traffic 2-4-0, No 7411, at Darlington, with enlarged cab, for working over the mountainous, storm-swept line to Tebay and Penrith.

Top right: Great Northern Railway: the 9.50am relief 'Scotsman' just north of Oakleigh Park Tunnel hauled by 4-4-2 No 1428. On the relief line a K2 Mogul is hauling a train of empty coaches from an excursion train.

Above right: One of the first two Gresley Pacifics, No 1471 *Sir Frederick Banbury* in Great Northern livery on the 1.30pm ex-Kings Cross, Leeds and Bradford express near Hadley Wood.

Right: One of the small boilered Great Northern Atlantics, No 3258, in the locomotive yard at Hitchin.

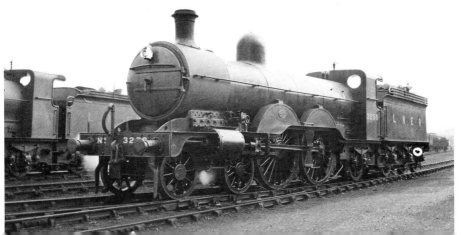

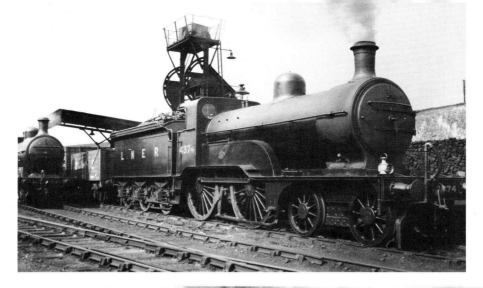

Top: An early Ivatt survival at Hitchin, 4-4-0 No 4374, (GNR No 1374) was one of a large class numbered from 1321 to 1385, built at Doncaster between 1898 and 1901. Apart from the substitution of Pop safety valves and the LNER style of painting this engine is unchanged from the original.

Above: Up express goods ascending the bank towards Stevenage. The engine is the second of the original GNR class of 3-cylinder 2-6-0s, which in LNER days were multiplied exceedingly to form Class K3.

6
Highland Fastnesses

In 1927, with a little judicious prodding from me, it was decided that the family holiday should be in the Highlands of Scotland. The difficulty was that my mother had very fixed ideas as to what constituted a suitable resort, while the accommodation had to be of the 'furnished rooms' type, where the landlady cooked the rations for which my mother went shopping locally. Additionally the resort had to have a traditional seafront. Eventually the choice fell upon Nairn, which if not boasting a grand esplanade of the Bournemouth or Torquay order had — far more delightful to me — a glorious view over the Moray Firth to the far mountains of Caithness. Our acccommodation, also, was an unexpected stroke of luck for me. One day, when I was very late back for high tea it was explained that I had gone to Culloden Moor taking photographs. The landlady was curious, and when it was explained that the subjects for my camera were trains, she went to a cupboard and bought out some vintage back numbers of *The Railway Magazine* — vintage years, when her father had been stationmaster at Nairn. She had been loath to destroy them and was only too glad for someone who was interested to take them away. Treasure trove indeed!

The rest of the family travelled to Nairn direct from Barrow, making various changes en route, and I went up from London for the middle fortnight of their month's stay. It would of course have been easy and logical to have used the Forres line portion of the 'Royal Highlander' from Euston, but that would have involved a long night's journey, with little opportunity for railway sightseeing; and so I went by the Midland 9.15pm sleeper from St Pancras, sitting up all night to log the running, and after a hearty breakfast in Edinburgh taking the 10.07am. Highland express by the North British route to Perth. On this latter we were hauled by one of the then new Scottish versions of the GCR 'Director' class, but named after characters in the Waverley novels, in this case *Lucy Ashton*. We broke no speed records on that run to Perth, but to me it was a delight, with my first sight and crossing of the Forth Bridge, the prospect over the historic Loch Leven, and a 70mph descent of Glen Farg. We carried through sections for both the Inverness direct line, and for Grantown, Forres, and Nairn. When we arrived at Perth a good deal of remarshalling was necessary to get the Glasgow and Edinburgh through carriages for each line into single groups, one on each side of the Pullman dining car, which was in the middle of the long train. We eventually had 13 vehicles, and I remember one coach of the Edinburgh-Nairn section was a typical Midland Clayton clerestory but painted to give the effect of varnished teak and lettered 'LNER'.

The combined train left Perth at 12 noon, and with such a load as 420 tons double-heading was inevitable. The 'Clan' class 4-6-0 engines, which were Class 4 in LMS reckoning, did take loads up to about 350 tons unassisted, on all but the three really severe sections. These were from Blair Atholl up to Dalnaspidal; from Inverness up to Slochd, and from Forres up to Dava summit. On all of these latter there were long gradients of 1 in 60-70, and the load limit was 220 tons tare. With our big train we had two 'Clans' throughout from Perth to Aviemore, *Clan Munro* and *Clan Mackinnon*. In 1927 all the Highland express engines were painted in Midland red, with the numbers, Derby fashion, in huge figures on their tenders. The majority of them were superbly clean, though naturally one regretted the passing of the old Highland style. It had, of course, become very drab before Grouping except in the case of a few engines like the second batch of 'Clans', which carried a very attractive leaf-green shade. In 1923 I had seen *Clan Mackinnon* at the time when Highland engines were working through to Glasgow Buchanan Street, and it looked a picture.

This latter, as train engine on the 12 noon from Perth in 1927 worked the Forres line portion of the train forward from Aviemore, and continued thus through to Inverness. The 'Direct Line' portion also of six coaches was, I recall, taken forward by one of the Large Ben type of 4-4-0s. Most engines of this class had been rebuilt with superheated boilers, but *Ben na Caillich*, stationed at Aviemore, retained her original boiler and the characteristic smokebox 'wings' in the traditional Drummond style. *Ben na Caillich* was one of the Highland engines that were afterwards sent to Kilmarnock for overhaul. She returned not only painted black but with the name spelt wrong, *Caillach*, to the disgust of the local enginemen, whose opinion of the Sassenach constituents of the LMS with which they were then associated plummeted to abysmal depths. In 1927 the 'black' era on the Highland had however not begun, and the only engine I saw other than goods types that were not red was one of the famous Jones Goods 4-6-0s which was still in Highland dark green and carrying its original number.

From Nairn I cycled across to Culloden Moor several times to see and photograph the procession of afternoon expresses to the south. It was a busy time on the up line. The four regular trains were the 3.45pm mail for Glasgow and Edinburgh, the 4.15pm 'Royal Highlander', for Euston, and the heavy 4.35pm which carried through sleeping car sections for both Euston and Kings Cross. These expresses were followed by the 5.20pm local train to Aviemore. The first two expresses ran non-stop from Inverness to Aviemore, while the third called at all stations by request. Often there was a relief to the 3.45pm. The latter connected with the 'North Mail' from Wick, and carried forward the TPO carriage. As far as I can remember it was the only regular carriage working north and south of Inverness. The Highland TPO vehicles had an interesting history. They were built during World War I to cope with the mail traffic occasioned by the basing of the Grand Fleet at Scapa Flow. There were three of them, and they were the first Highland postal vans to have the traductor apparatus for picking up and setting down the pouches at speed. They worked continuously on the mail trains for 45 years.

The three regular southbound expresses, 3.45, 4.15, and 4.35pm from Inverness all loaded to more than 220 tons for a 'Clan' class engine, and required piloting daily. The Highland never had any engines to spare in the summer tourist season, and at Inverness an ingenious way of providing assistance for these trains was adopted. The through engines, working to Perth, would be starting 'cold', and in such conditions the initial bank at 1 in 60 up to Culloden Moor could be a killer; but three connecting trains arrived in Inverness not long previously, and the engines from these were coaled and watered, remanned, and used as pilots for the southbound trains up to Slochd summit. Thus the engine newly arrived from Kyle of Lochalsh, usually a 'Jones Goods', or a Cumming goods 4-6-0 piloted the mail; the 4-4-0 which had worked the Aberdeen train from Keith, coupled on to the Euston 'sleeper', while the engine that had come down from Wick on the 'North Mail', always a 'Castle', was available for the 4.35pm — usually the heaviest train of the three. For the record, some engine combinations I noted in 1927 were:

1st Day
3.45pm Jones Goods and *Cawdor Castle*
4.15pm *Ben Loyal* and *Clan Stewart*
4.35pm Brodie Castle and *Clan Munro*
2nd Day
3.45pm Cumming Goods and *Brahan Castle*
4.15pm *Loch Ruthven* and *Gordon Castle*
4.35pm *Murthly Castle* and *Clan Cameron*

What a feast for the observer, and there was another treat to follow, because about an hour after the last of these trains had toiled up the bank the three pilots came back, coupled together, each running tender first. The Aviemore 'stopper' was usually worked by a 'Large Ben' class 4-4-0, often the non-superheated *Ben na Caillich*.

The scene was no less animated at Aviemore in the late afternoon. The 2.30pm from Inverness to the south, via Forres, carried through sections for Edinburgh and Glasgow. This train arrived at Aviemore just ahead of the 3.45 from Inverness and a general remarshalling took place to make up two separate trains. That for Glasgow, with the TPO van went first, having attached also the Pullman dining car that had come north on the 12 noon from Perth. The Edinburgh train, worked by the engine that had brought the 2.30pm round via Forres, followed at 5.10pm. The long climb up to Drumochter summit is not so severely graded on the northern side, and both these trains frequently left unpiloted, although loaded to over 300 tons. When I went south by the Edinburgh train at the end of my 1927 holiday a load of 295 tons was taken by *Clan Campbell*, and good time was kept throughout. Appropos of piloting the Mail out of Inverness, on one of our expeditions farther west, by hired car, I contrived that we were on the road between Garve and Loch Luichart, near Corriemuille summit, about the time the midday train up from Kyle of Lochalsh was due; and to my delight she came up hauled not by one of the goods 4-6-0s but by one of the little 'Skye bogie' 4-4-0s, most regally clean in Midland red. I often wondered if she was put on to double-head the Mail from Inverness to Slochd later that afternoon.

In 1927 4-4-0 engines were still in regular use on the Kyle road. Later that same day I saw one of the 'Loch' class 4-4-0s taking a mixed freight train westwards, pounding vigorously up the 1 in 50 gradient from the station. On a day trip from Inverness to Kyle of Lochalsh and back we were hauled by a Cumming's 4-6-0, sometimes referred to as the 'Clan Goods', though actually their introduction preceded the 'Clan' class passenger engines by about a year. The load was not heavy and the engine climbed that back-breaking 4 miles up at 1 in 50 from Fodderty Junction to the Raven Rock without assistance; but when I travelled that way a few years later we had Cumming goods 4-6-0s front and rear up this formidable incline. The turntable and its approaches at Kyle of Lochalsh, in a recess blasted out of the solid rock, has provided the setting for many a Highland locomotive portrait; but none can surely have graced it more brilliantly than the 4-4-0 engine *Loch Garve* which I found there and photographed in the autumn of 1927. The engine, beautifully turned out in Midland red, and lit by the late afternoon sun was indeed a picture.

The family holiday at Nairn was repeated in the following year, but railway wise it was surprising how many changes were to be seen in a mere 12 months. The first hit me hard the moment we reached Perth, to continue as before on the 12 noon express. The train engine was the *Clan Mackinnon* as on my earlier trip, but the pilot was a new Midland type 0-6-0 goods engine. Chiefly in helping the 'Clan' to make quicker starts from rest, this new and unlikely engine assisted in effecting slightly better overall times; but my recollection is mainly of the continuous roar from the front end on the faster stretches. On the long climb from Struan up to Dalnaspidal the times of both the 1927 and the 1928 runs were almost identical. Curiously enough this opening journey was the only occasion in the whole fortnight in the Highlands that I saw one of these Midland 0-6-0s. As a pilot she would not have needed to be specially equipped to work over the line, because the mechanical tablet exchanging at the various loops was performed by the train engine.

One other thing I saw at once, and it saddened me, was a marked deterioration in the external condition of many of the engines. By 1928 the edict had gone forth on the LMS that all except the top line express passenger engines were to be painted black, and because this did not include any of the former Highland engines many of them had already been repainted. The psychological effect of this change on the locomotive men in the north seems to have been little short of catastrophic. Many of the main line express engines were in a state of absolute filth, looking all the worse where the cab sides had been given a perfunctory rub with a cloth to reveal the number. To see engines like the 'Clans' and 'Castles' which had been the pride and joy of Inverness in such a state was depressing in the extreme. Such engines as remained in red were reasonably clean, but nothing to compare with the splendour of their appearance a year earlier. There did not seem to be any appreciable falling off in the quality of the running; in fact some of the journeys I made in several directions out of Inverness gave me smart times, particularly by 'Castle' class engines, including the highest maximum speed I ever noted with an engine of Highland design. A speed of 67mph down a gradient of 1 in 60 would not appear to be anything very wonderful, but maxima in excess of 60 were not frequent.

The principal interest in the locomotive working during 1928 however was the transfer of the six 'River' class 4-6-0s from the Caledonian to the Highland section; and although being designated Class 4 under LMS management and thus having the same load limits as the 'Clans' their addition to the motive power stud was very welcome. At the time it was said that their transfer to the line for which they were originally designed was because certain bridges had been strengthened, and their heavier axle loading could accordingly be accepted. But this was not the case at all. F. G. Smith designed the 'River' class engines very skilfully, so arranging their balancing that although they had considerably higher axle loads than the 'Castles', the hammer blow, or dynamic augment at speed was much less. Accordingly the overall effect of the locomotives on the track and underline bridges was no more severe than that of the 'Castles'. But there had been some unpleasantness among the senior officers of the Highland Railway, and the situation between Smith and the civil engineer, Alexander Newlands was difficult, to put it mildly. There have been several stories as to how the 'River' class engines came to be banned from doing *any* running on the Highland; but banned they were, and Smith was given a week to resign, or be dismissed.

So those six splendid engines, of which the Highland were in sore need in 1915, were sold to the Caledonian. The latter company never seemed to appreciate their sterling worth, and used them mainly on fast goods trains between Carlisle and Perth, whereas they were without much doubt the best *express passenger* engines the Caledonian ever had. Then, after World War I there was set up the Bridge Stress Committee, in 1923. Although its report was not published until 1929, its findings were well enough known among railway engineers well before that date. The remit of the Committee was ably prefaced by Earl Balfour at the time of its publication, thus:

'The interaction between bridge and locomotive is the root of the matter. Yet no maker of locomotives is greatly concerned with structure of bridges, nor has the builder of bridges possessed adequate opportunities of experimenting with locomotives in motion. The complex relation between the two has therefore never been completely understood, not could it be until the need for a cooperative effort became fully realised.'

Smith understood the problem well enough and designed the 'River' class engines accordingly; but human relations were such that the Civil Engineer just did not want to know. The 'Rivers' were one of the engine classes analysed by the Bridge Stress Committee, with the result that they were found to be considerably less severe on the track and bridges than the 'Clans', which the Civil Engineer had accepted in 1919. So, even before the report of the Bridge Stress Committee was published the 'Rivers' were transferred on to the Highland Line. They did much excellent work, and I wish I had been able to continue south from Aviemore on the up Mail on 1 September 1928. Engine No 14758, which on the Highland should have been 72 *River Tay*, was on the job from Inverness, but with a tare load of 269 tons a pilot had to be taken up to Slochd, on that day the *Clan Chattan*. It was easy for two engines, and then No 14758 ran the downhill 11.9 miles to Aviemore in just 15min, start to stop, with a maximum speed of $63\frac{1}{2}$mph.

I had gone to Aviemore to take photographs and watched the remarshalling of the Glasgow sections from the Forres line and from our own train, and then saw, to my interest and making a splendid picture, the 'River' start away unassisted with a load of about 350 tons. Long after she had passed I could hear the roar of her exhaust climbing the first stretch of 1 in 150 gradient out of Aviemore. I was sorry not to have been travelling south that day. At Aviemore I saw for the first time, and photographed one of the 'Loch' class engines that had been rebuilt with a Caledonian boiler. It was not a pretty sight. I can quite understand that by 1927-8 spare boilers of the original 'Loch' type would have been few and far between, and no new ones would have been made. So that when engines of this class were sent south for repairs and the boilers needed renewal St Rollox, or Kilmarnock put on the nearest they had that would fit. But in the case of *Loch Insh*, as with several others they put on short Pickersgill type chimneys, while retaining the original height of dome cover, as happened with some of the indigenous Caledonian engines too, and the result was horrible.

Some years later one of the rebuilt 'Lochs' was the subject of a good laugh at Euston. In the later 1930s a semi-technical journalist from across the Atlantic succeeded in getting the entrée to the footplate in Great Britain. He was a first rate, if somewhat verbose raconteur, but was apt to get his facts somewhat mixed up, and to jump to conclusions. But his articles always made excellent reading. He was however inclined to take a rather high handed view of the routine required by the public relations departments of the railways, in return for the privileges granted, and used to try and circumvent their authority by writing direct to chief mechanical engineers, and other high officers. Well, one day I went into the offices at Euston, and found them virtually rolling on the floor, over a manuscript that had just come into their hands from this man. Apparently he had ridden north from Perth on a Stanier 'Black-Five', and at Blair Atholl the pilot provided to give assistance up 'The Hill' was, I quote 'a Caledonian "Dunalastair" that someone had rebuilt with outside cylinders'!

Towards the end of that 1928 holiday I went up to Slochd with the intention of photographing the congregation of pilots in the late afternoon before they returned to Inverness; but I was completely thwarted. I duly photographed the 3.45pm with *Clan Cameron* and *Clan Chattan* pounding their way up the last mile of 1 in 60, but when I got up to the summit I found that the train had not stopped, and both engines had gone on to Aviemore. I found a suitable vantage point in that rather grim defile, and waited for the 4.15pm, meantime the light was getting progressively worse. In due course, to my surprise, all signals were pulled off and when the Euston 'sleeper' did come she too ran through without dropping her pilot — *Loch Laoghal* and *Murthly Castle*. The only one of the three that did shed its pilot was the 4.35, and by that time the light was bad, and the engines so dirty that photography was just not on.

The pilot of the 4.15pm then carrying the original type of boiler, was another of those Highland engines that had its name misspelt after Grouping. One can have plenty of sympathy for the Sassenachs who had to paint such tongue-twisting names on to these engines from the north, and in this case *Laoghal* was rendered *Laochal*. As far as I could see it beneath the grime it was the latter as it passed me at Slochd that September day. The loch in question is up in the wilds of Sutherlandshire, in the shadow of the mountain of the same name; but when Peter Drummond brought out his first class of inside cylinder 4-4-0s, named after mountains, he played safe and used the phonetic spelling on engine No 15, *Ben Loyal*. The 'Small Bens', built entirely in the Drummond tradition, were splendid little engines, although at first their crews strongly disapproved of their having inside cylinders and Stephenson link motion, instead of Allan's straight link gear. The 'Small Bens' were much in evidence through Nairn on the Inverness-Aberdeen trains. I went through to Keith one afternoon and *Ben Vrackie* put in some excellent work, with a load of 175 tons.

The 'Small Bens' were built in Glasgow by Dübs & Co, and our landlady at Nairn having heard of my interest in locomotives showed me a large official photograph taken at the builders' works of No 1 named *Ben Nevis*; but apparently objection was raised in high quarters to having a Highland engine named after a mountain, however great, that was in exclusively North British territory, and No 1 was renamed *Ben Y-Gloe* even before it left Glasgow. Although having roughly the same nominal tractive effort the 'Small Bens' never seemed to have quite the 'guts' of the outside cylindered 'Lochs' and in their earlier days they worked mainly on the further north main line, on which the hard gradients, although as steep in places, were not nearly so long as those south of Inverness. Nevertheless *Ben Attow* was one that I noted on main line piloting work from Aviemore in September 1928.

Despite dirty engines the spirit of the old Highland Railway still prevailed in 1928, and I am glad to have seen it then, when the one alien note in a fortnight's observation and travelling was that Midland 0-6-0 piloted my train from Perth to Aviemore on the very first day. When I next went that way in 1931 all was changing and our train engine from Perth was a Horwich Mogul.

Top: The 4.35pm from Inverness to London, in 1927, with through sleeping car portions for both Euston and Kings Cross, here seen near Daviot, climbing a 1 in 60 gradient. The engines, *Brodie Castle* and *Clan Munro* were both painted in Midland red at the time.

Centre: The Nairn and Forres line section of the combined Euston and Kings Cross 'sleeper', on Dava Moor, dreaded for its winter snow blocks, hauled by 'Big Ben' class 4-4-0 No 14419 *Ben Mholach*. This was an unusual working, because of a temporary shortage of engines at Inverness. A washout at Brora had trapped a number of engines north of the breach.

Above: One of the 'River' class 4-6-0s at Aviemore, in 1928, after they had been returned to the Highland after a 12-year exile on the Caledonian.

Left: In 1928, one of the 'Loch' class 4-4-0s that were rebuilt with Caledonian type boilers photographed at Aviemore, painted in Midland red, and carrying its LMS number in large numerals on the tender, *Loch Insh* was originally HR No 119.

Below: Winter at Aviemore: a Drummond 'Barney' 0-6-0 goods, and a rebuilt 'Loch', both equipped with snow ploughs.

Bottom: One of the two 4-4-0s built by C. Cumming in 1916 for working the mail trains between Inverness and Wick. In 1928 when photographed at Inverness, No 14523 *Durn*, had been painted plain black.

Top: An historic station pilot at Inverness in 1927. This engine was originally built in 1879, as a 2-4-0T, and named *Highlander*. It was rebuilt as a 4-4-0T in 1885, but the name was removed in 1900. At the time of Grouping it was renumbered 59A, but it was then repainted in red and numbered 15010. In 1927 it was looking rather shop-soiled.

Above: Inverness yard looking east, with engine No 14692 *Darnaway Castle* taking water.

Right: Bringing up the mail from Kyle of Lochalsh. A 'Skye bogie', No 14284 in red, out on the moors near Loch Luichart.

Top: In the small rock-girt engine yard at Kyle of Lochalsh, in 1927: a resplendent *Loch Garve*, one of three engines of this type built in 1917 for the war traffic.

Above: Another smart 4-4-0 at the Kyle: No 14416 of the 'Small Ben' class; *Ben a 'Bhuird* (HR No 47) was the last of this excellent class, and was built by the North British Locomotive Co in 1906.

Below: One of Cumming's mixed traffic 4-6-0s, sometimes called the 'Clan Goods'. These engines were doing most of the passenger work on the Kyle road in 1927-32. No 17953 was built in 1918.

7
North Eastern: A Largely Unchanged Scene

By the early 1930s the railway scene over much of Great Britain was changing rapidly. Over most of the LMS Midlandisation was in full blast; main line electrification had begun on the Southern, and on the Great Western most of the much-loved 6ft 8½in 4-4-0s had been replaced by new mixed traffic 4-6-0s. In the Southern Area of the LNER rebuildings were changing the look of many Great Eastern engines while 'flowerpot' chimneys were disfiguring those of the Great Central. To lovers of the traditional therefore it was heartening to travel north of York. True, there were plenty of Gresley Pacifics about, and some D49 class 3-cylinder 4-4-0s; but except for veterans like the express passenger 2-4-0s, and the 4-2-2 singles, the stud as I knew it 10 years earlier was virtually intact, and, best of all, unchanged in appearance. No one at Darlington Works, fortunately, seemed to think it was the 'done thing' to put on Pacific-sized dome covers and 'flowerpot' chimneys, and North Eastern express passenger, and freight locomotives retained their original handsome outlines. During 1932 and 1933 I was able to make some extensive explorations in the North Eastern Area, and the locomotive and train working was a delight to observe.

The Raven 3-cylinder Atlantics of Class Z, which under the LNER classification became C7 were to me one of the most elegant of pre-Grouping passenger locomotives. There was something in the broadside view of their action, of the coupling and connecting rods, derived from the drive on to the leading coupled axle, and the soft 'purr' of their rapid exhaust beats, six to each revolution. Furthermore, when I first became a regular reader of *The Railway Magazine* the articles by the late Cecil J. Allen contained notes of many runs with these engines conveying perfectly colossal loads, without assistance. Admittedly the speeds were not very high on the gradual rising length from York to Northallerton; but the mere fact of these engines starting away from York with trains of well over 500 tons was enough to excite the imagination of anyone interested in locomotive performance. Then, in 1921, when the evening Glasgow-Leeds dining car express was accelerated to a 43min run from Darlington to York, taking up the timing of the one-time fastest train in the British Empire with a considerably heavier load, the Zs showed they could run at 80mph on level track.

The mechanical design of the Z class became the subject of enhanced interest after Grouping. The North Eastern locomotive department under the direction of Sir Vincent Raven had adopted 3-cylinder propulsion in a big way, but in a strikingly different form from that which Gresley was developing on the Great Northern. The Doncaster principle was to make everything about the machinery readily get-at-able, using only two sets of Walschaerts valve gear, and the valves of the middle cylinder actuated by a system of conjugate levers across the front end of the engine. Raven on the other hand used three sets of Stephenson's link motion, all between the frames. This fundamental difference between the 3-cylinder express locomotives of the Great Northern and North Eastern Railways was the subject of much comment when Gresley read a paper at the summer meeting of the Institution of Mechanical Engineers in Railway Centenary year, 1925. Sir Vincent Raven, as President of the Institution was in the chair, and he wound up an interesting discussion by saying, I quote from the proceedings: 'he always adhered to the Stephenson valve gear, as he believed in simplicity. He used the three sets of valve gear, and if he went back to railwork today, he would do the same again'.

Gresley, in his reply to the discussion treated the matter somewhat cavalierly. The is reported thus: 'He thanked the President for his remarks. They all had their own opinions as to whether it was better to have two or three valve gears. He knew that Sir Vincent preferred the Stephenson gears and preferably three. It was obvious, being in Darlington, the home of Stephenson, that the Stephenson valve gear must be used there'.

The Gresley Pacifics allocated to the North Eastern Area were nearly all stationed at Gateshead, with a few at Heaton. There were not all that many of them, as they had to cover workings northward to Edinburgh, southwards to York and Leeds, and half the double-home turns between Newcastle and Kings Cross. They were not very thick on the ground, and when any of the regular trains were run in duplicate the relief sections were worked by ex-NER Atlantics. Some important regular trains were also taken by Zs such as the Pullmans, between Leeds and Newcastle, via Harrogate, and various Saturdays only expresses in high summer. Quite apart from the lighter-loaded 'star' trains there were many semi-fasts that were Atlantic hauled, this last category included the two-cylinder V class engines (LNER) Class C6. These latter, although very massive and impressive machines never seemed to me to have the speed and freedom in running as the Zs. It was probably due to the valve setting, and not to any inherent differences from 2-, or 3-cylinder propulsion.

A secondary route that I found great interest in exploring was that from Newcastle to Carlisle. It was, of course, one of the earliest railways in the entire country, and the first to go right across from east to west. On more than one occasion it has provided a vitally important relief route to the East Coast main line in cases of dire emergency; but before recalling what happened in the summer of 1947, for example, a little outside the period of this book in any case, I must tell how I saw it under normal working conditions. In 1933, when I spent several long weekends in the delightful country beside the upper Tyne, there was very little infiltration of post-Grouping types of locomotive. It was almost pure North Eastern. There were then 10 through trains in each direction between Newcastle and Carlisle. The best of these stopped only at Blaydon, Stocksfield, Hexham and Haltwhistle while during the night the Stranraer boat expresses ran non-stop over the $60\frac{3}{4}$ miles of the route in 80-82min. Apart from this latter all the ordinary trains were made up of ex-North Eastern non-corridor stock and the loads rarely exceeded eight coaches.

For the most part passenger trains, both stopping and otherwise, were hauled by ex-North Eastern 4-4-0s, usually of the Q (LNER Class D17) and R (LNER Class D20) classes. From the Carlisle end one sometimes saw ex-North British superheated 4-4-0s of the 'Scott' class, and Gresley 3-cylinder Moguls of Class K3. In the years before World War I North Eastern Atlantics used to work across to Carlisle, and I have seen it suggested that the locomotive authorities of the NER sent them there for prestige purposes. The Citadel station was then a parade ground for the largest locomotives of the five companies engaged in the Anglo-Scottish traffic through Carlisle and it was thought that the North Eastern ought to show the flag to a greater extent than by using 2-4-0s and small 4-4-0s, which were all that were actually necessary to work the light trains then operated. This was not really the true explanation. The top link express passenger engines at Gateshead, then mostly Atlantics together with the large R1 4-4-0s (LNER Class D21), were all making extensive weekly mileages. They were all double-manned, and an engine that had been to Edinburgh and back, would change one of its regular crews for the second, and go to York and back, to Leeds via the coast route, and then Harrogate, or in some cases to Carlisle. With the introduction of the Gresley Pacifics, and the double-home turns between Newcastle and Kings Cross, the regular working of Gateshead top link engines to Carlisle had ceased. Ex-NER Atlantics continued to run this particular road, though in a secondary capacity. Very occasionally ex-North British Atlantics would work across from Carlisle.

The local trains were equally a preserve of ex-North Eastern engines. The most numerous between Hexham and Newcastle were the Class O (LNER Class G5) 0-4-4Ts, which were very smart little jobs. Among my old notes I find reference to working of the Raven 3-cylinder 4-4-4Ts formerly known as Class D, but H1 under the LNER classification. Those engines were later converted to 4-6-2Ts, and replaced the Worsdell inside-cylinder 4-6-2Ts of NER Class W, on the heavily graded Saltburn to Scarborough line. All the ex-North Eastern engines, not excepting the local tanks, and freight types, were very comfortably appointed in their cabs. In later years I had a number of footplate rides on the 0-4-4Ts, and found them delightfully free and smooth running engines. When I wrote my book devoted entirely to the locomotives of the North Eastern Railway, in 1954, there were still about a hundred of them still in regular service.

Another ex-NER class of which I have pleasant memories, and which were to be seen on the Newcastle and Carlisle line in 1933 on both passenger and goods train, was the Class C 0-6-0 (LNER Class J21). Many of them were built originally as Worsdell-Von Borries 2-cylinder compounds; but at the time I knew them they had 19in by 24in cylinders and superheater boilers. They were splendid little engines. So far as cab comfort was concerned I always remember finding one of them in the small locomotive yard at Penrith. Mac Pearson and I were then hunting down old North Western engines and had been delighted to find a 2-4-0 'Jumbo' *Tartarus* on shed, albeit in a somewhat woe-begone condition. There were also several of the 18in 'Cauliflower' 0-6-0s. The difference between their stark, excessively austere cab interiors, and the wood-panelled elegance of the North Eastern Class C was positively stunning.

Locomotives that were much sought after by photographers, and by those compiling logs of fast train running, were the five Raven type Pacifics. These engines always seemed to me to be a rather hurried counterblast to the production of the first two Gresley Pacifics for Great Northern Railway in the spring of 1922. The two railways were to be merged at the end of the year, under the Grouping scheme, and one can sense that Sir Vincent Raven, although due for retirement, was not prepared to leave the scene with the Great Northern undisputably the largest and most powerful passenger engine in the new Group. The intention to build a North Eastern Pacific was announced long before the first of the engines was actually completed at Darlington Works, and a line drawing and basic dimensions were published in the July 1922 issue of *The Railway Magazine*. When the first of the new engines did appear it was seen to be a much enlarged and elongated edition of the very successful Z class 3-cylinder Atlantic, except that the firebox was of the wide type. In comparative tests conducted between Doncaster and Kings Cross in the summer of 1923 there proved to be not a great deal of difference between the Gresley and Raven types of 4-6-2 as the former then were. The differences were however just enough to justify the adoption of the Gresley type as an LNER standard.

After the A1 class had their valve gear modified, and their coal consumption greatly reduced there was no comparison between the two types of Pacific, though for a time the Raven engines continued to work important trains, chiefly north of Newcastle. They never worked on the long double-home turns to and from Kings Cross. On the north main line I saw them working not only on semi-fast trains, but on first class turns like the 1.20pm ex-Kings Cross, north of Newcastle, the up 'Queen of Scots' Pullman, and I logged No 2401 on the up 'Flying Scotsman' as far south as Newcastle in 1932. At one time the engine of the 'Queen of Scots' Pullman worked through from Edinburgh to Leeds, but as I saw No 2402 only as she passed Tweedmouth I cannot say if she did so on this 1932 occasion. There seemed a degree of uncertainty in their regular workings north of Newcastle. I remember how disappointed Mac Pearson was on one bank holiday week trip we spent together in the neighbourhood of Berwick-on-Tweed. I had been out on my own on the Saturday, before he joined me, and had 'bagged' three out of the five NER Pacifics. On the Monday we did not see a single one, and then it was only on the train that we both had to take on the Tuesday that No 2401 turned up!

Pacifics apart however, the north main line, as it was known in railway circles in the north-east, was a source of intense interest to anyone seeking out the former North Eastern locomotives. On the heaviest trains, of course, the Gresley Pacifics were omniscient. One looked out for the non-stop in each direction, and No 4472 *Flying Scotsman* came through in one direction or the other every day. At the time of which I am now writing the most usual balancing engine from Edinburgh was No 2795 *Call Boy*. The 'Junior Scotsman', following the 'non-stop', was always a heavy train, worked by Gateshead Pacifics, but a surprising number of other first class express duties were regularly worked by the Z Atlantics, both from the Gateshead and the Edinburgh end. If a Pacific was not available for a turn like the up 'Junior Scotsman' loading to over 500 tons it would be worked by two Atlantics. When double-heading was required from the Newcastle end the assistant engine was usually a Class R 4-4-0, and in such cases the North Eastern followed North British practice in putting the train engine in the lead, and the 'assistant' next to the train. This of course was a far more logical arrangement than that customary on the Midland and the London and North Western, which always put the pilots in front. I must admit that it would have looked very strange to see a 'Claughton' leading a 2-4-0 'Jumbo', but no stranger than one occasion when I photographed the up 'Flying Scotsman' (winter service) at Marshall Meadows, north of Berwick, and it was hauled by a Gresley A1 Pacific heading an ex-Great Northern superheater 4-4-0 of the 50 class (LNER Class 'DI') The North Eastern and Scottish areas of the LNER were quite strict in the load limits fixed for Pacifics in regard to the Cockburnspath bank, even after the streamlined A4s had come upon the scene.

The most interesting and exciting Z working during the period of the summer service in 1933 was that of the 6.38pm down from Newcastle to Edinburgh. This, of course, was the 1.20pm from Kings Cross, the load of which was reduced from the usual 15 or 16, to 10 coaches at Newcastle. It was a Haymarket turn, and during the period of the summer service and the need to provide the best Pacific on hand for the 'non-stop', the Scottish Region was definitely short of big engines. The balancing turn for the 6.38pm down from Newcastle was in intermediate express leaving Edinburgh ahead of the up afternoon Scotsman, 2.05pm from Waverley. This latter was normally a Pacific turn, but the engine worked through to York, and was not available immediately for a return duty. This did not always work out. One day when I was travelling on this train through to Kings Cross the Pacific was in trouble for steam, and we stopped at Tweedmouth to take the up East Coast pilot, to help us get to Newcastle. A Z coupled on ahead of the ailing Pacific, and her driver seemed to tear into it with a relish, helping to regain quite a lot of the time we had lost down from Edinburgh. Far from continuing to York two more Zs were waiting to take the train forward from Newcastle.

The 6.38pm down had some sharp point-to-point timings, and with a daily load of about 320 tons tare, needed some had work from Atlantic engines. During a holiday at Berwick in the summer of 1933 I used to walk out to the cliffs south of Tweedmouth to see her coming tearing up the 1 in 190 gradient past Scremerston. They always seemed to be going very hard, with quite a roar from the exhaust, and looking up the timetable I found they were booked to cover the 32 miles from Alnmouth Junction to Berwick in 36min start to stop. Considering they had a lengthy uphill start up the Loughoughton bank, before they could really get going this was quite a stiff booking. Once or twice I made an afternoon trip to Alnmouth to sample the work and found it as interesting as I expected. With engine No 729 and a load of 340 tons it took $9\frac{1}{2}$min to climb the 4.6 miles of 1 in 170 from the start to Little Mill, and then we went like the wind. Over the 17.8 miles from Christon bank to Goswick speed averaged 69mph, with a maximum of $76\frac{1}{2}$mph, at Beal, and with a tremendous finish up on the cliffs at Scremerston we clocked into Berwick on time — but only just. It was a mighty tough job, and those Atlantics, driven hard as they were, did not always keep strict time.

Tweedmouth shed was a very interesting place in those days. They always had an Atlantic standing pilot, ready to assist or take over any train at a moments notice; but in addition to that there was always a fascinating variety of engines on shed. Of tank engines there were examples of both the 2-4-2 Worsdell A class, and the 0-4-4Ts, while 4-4-0s of the R and the M class were regularly working on local trains. It was particularly interesting to find the M class engine No 1621, which participated in the record running between York and Edinburgh on the last night of the Race to the North, in 1895. There were the ubiquitous J21 class 0-6-0 goods engines, and also the big Raven 3-cylinder 4-6-0s of Class S3, which worked some of the fast goods turns. Tweedmouth shed provided some of the power for the Border Union line to Kelso, and there were often some ex-North British engines, big superheated 0-6-0 goods, and an occasional 'Scott' class 4-4-0. For the most part that shed yard had a wholly pre-Grouping atmosphere, though one day I did find one of the Gresley D49 class 3-cylinder 4-4-0s of the 'Shire' series.

In the years 1933 and 1934 the work of the V and Z class Atlantics on the numerous weekend relief trains continued to be very good, with train loads up to about 350 tons. They were not required to run very hard south of Newcastle. The standard non-stop time northbound was then 92min start to stop for the 80.1 miles, taking 48min for the first 44.1 miles from York to passing Darlington. There was some closely pathed timing from York, immediately after the passage of the non-stop 'Flying Scotsman' at 1.29pm. There followed, at 1.34pm a

Glasgow express that originated at York, followed immediately by two sections of the 10.05am 'Junior Scotsman' from Kings Cross. Then, at 1.55pm came the Liverpool-Newcastle express. The main part of the 'Junior Scotsman' was a regular Pacific double-home turn from Kings Cross to Newcastle; but the others were regular Atlantic jobs, and at different times I sampled all three. On the 1.34pm with a Class V (LNER Class C6) No 649 and a load of 305 tons we were running close on the tail of the 'non-stop', which was allowed 91min pass to pass from York to Newcastle but did not seem to be doing very well that day. We sighted adverse signals from it four times, and with two permanent way checks in addition took $94\frac{3}{4}$min to Newcastle.

On the second part of the 10.50am a Z, No 2210, hauling 340 tons, was similarly handicapped by the presence of the very heavy first portion just ahead, though the driver coaxed his engine to some vigorous spurts intermediately, and we were able to keep end to end time — actually $91\frac{1}{2}$min. But with a clear road we could have made the run in 85min. By far the most exciting was a run on the Liverpool train behind engine No 710, class Z, and a load of 315 tons. With a clear road, and going hard throughout we passed Thirsk, 22.2 miles, in $23\frac{1}{4}$min at 72mph on the level; Northallerton, 30 miles, in exactly even time, and Croft Spa, 41.5 miles in 40min at 75mph. We should have completed the 44.1 miles to the stop at Darlington in $43\frac{1}{2}$min but for a signal stop just outside. The Zs however were not at their best in hard hillclimbing. I was on that 1.34pm relief one day north of Newcastle with engine No 733 and a 350 ton load. We did well as far as Berwick, covering that 66.9 miles from Newcastle in $75\frac{1}{2}$min start to stop, instead of the 80min scheduled, with running north of Alnmouth that was practically up to the exacting standards of the 1.20pm from Kings Cross. But a very laborious climb up to Burnmouth followed, and we dropped $3\frac{1}{2}$min to passing Dunbar. This loss was however practically recovered by the time we were approaching Edinburgh, though adverse signals robbed us of a punctual arrival.

My last recollection of the former North Eastern engines, and particularly of the 3-cylinder types is of hump marshalling yards. It was J. G. Robinson of the Great Central who first demonstrated the efficacy of a heavy 3-cylinder tank engine for shunting work over the steep gradients of a hump marshalling yard. He had introduced massive 0-8-4T engines for use at Wath, in 1907, and faced with a similar duty in the big Erimus yard beside the River Tees, near Middlesbrough, Wilson Worsdell built the first North Eastern 3-cylinder simple locomotives, a powerful 4-8-0 design, known as Class X (LNER Class T1). These engines of which 10 were built originally in 1909-1910 were very successful in propelling trains over the humps, and a further five were built by the LNER after Grouping in 1925. I became very familiar with their working, not at Erimus but in the new hump marshalling yard at Hessle, near Hull, which was brought into service in 1935. I was concerned with the design and manufacture of some of the special machinery for that yard, and spent a good deal of time there observing the operation. Some of the busiest times were during the night hours, and then I had to observe the humping operations, and occasionally photograph the locomotives under the floodlights in the yard.

Top: North Eastern, up mail train, with TPO carriage Edinburgh to York, leaving the Royal Border Bridge at Berwick: 3-cylinder Z class Atlantic No 718.

Above: One of the ex-NER Class V 2-cylinder Atlantics (LNER Class C6) No 703 at Darlington.

Right: Down relief East Coast express recovering from permanent way slowing at Wiske Moor Troughs north of Northallerton, hauled by 3-cylinder Atlantic No 735 Class Z (LNER Class C7).

Top: An historic North Eastern 4-4-0 No 1621, which ran the Aberdeen racing train from York to Newcastle in August 1895, here photographed at Tweedmouth, in 1933. This engine is now preserved in the National Railway Museum at York.

Above: An interesting assembly in Tweedmouth roundhouse, 1932: engines left to right are Class P3 0-6-0 No 2349; Class A 2-4-2T No 483; a North British 0-6-0 superheater goods; a Class A 2-4-2T, and a Class E 0-6-0T.

Top right: A Raven 3-cylinder mixed traffic 4-6-0, NER Class S3, No 911 (LNER Class B16) at Tweedmouth in 1933.

Above right: A Wordsell Class A 2-4-2T No 483 (LNER Class F8) at Tweedmouth in 1933.

Right: Down intermediate express leaving Berwick for Edinburgh in 1932, hauled by the first of the Raven Pacifics No 2400 *City of Newcastle.*

Top: A night scene at Hull Inwards Yard with one of the 3-cylinder 4-8-0T engines posed on the crest of the hump, after propelling a train into the classification sidings.

Centre: An express excursion train, Carlisle to Newcastle, passing Bardon Mill, hauled by 0-6-0 engine No 1339 Class C (LNER Class J21).

Above: One of the ex-NER Class T 0-8-0s (LNER Class Q5) No 1709 at Darlington. This engine was one of 10 built at Gateshead works in 1902, with slide valves, instead of Smith's segmental piston valves, used on other engines of the class. Another 40 engines of the the slide valve variety were built later, and the whole 50 saw war service in France with the Railway Operating Division.

8
LMS: Early Stanier Days

Until my father retired from business at the end of 1930, and with my own professional work based in London I led a somewhat nomadic existence, carrying the minimum of effects at successive temporary quarters while the bulk of my growing collection of books, papers, photographs and other impedimenta was at home, in Barrow. Then, after various explorations in the Home Counties the family home became established at Bushey, and I became a commuter between Watford Junction and Euston. Bushey and Oxhey was very much our nearest station, but I always had a season ticket to Watford so as to take advantage of a fast non-stop train to Euston in the mornings. While as a journalist and author I have always striven to be impartial, I think that if I had a favourite among the pre-Grouping railways it was the London and North Western, despite an alleged partiality towards the Great Western that has followed me through life. In view of earlier sentiments therefore it was with more than usual interest that I began an almost day by day scrutiny of the southern and of the West Coast route.

At the end of 1930 the great transition had scarcely begun. The period of intense Midlandisation that followed Sir Henry Fowler's appointment to succeed Hughes as Chief Mechanical Engineer had largely 'blown itself out', as the weather men might say. The 'Royal Scot' class 4-6-0s were well entrenched, but were not at first proving the wonders they were first made out to be, and the Midland compounds were confined almost entirely to the Birmingham and Wolverhampton service. Elsewhere the ex-LNWR engines were carrying on. The 'Claughtons' in particular were called upon for much heavy and important work, as understudies to the 'Royal Scots', and regular turns in 1930-1 included the up 'Merseyside Express', the down 'Lancastrian' at 6.05pm from Euston, and the up 'Midday Scot' between Crewe and Euston. From my observations the punctuality was good. The 'Prince of Wales' class was less in evidence, but there was a good reason for this which I did not discover until many years later. We had an excellent train up from Watford in the mornings, allowed only 21min, start to stop for 17.5miles to Euston. Its minimum load was one of nine coaches, six of these modern corridor stock, and making a load of 285 tons. On this train 'Prince of Wales' and 'George the Fifth' class engines from Bletchley shed gave some sparkling performances daily, taking little more than 20min for the run, and usually attaining maximum speeds of around 73 or 74mph at Wembley.

Previous to this time 20 of the 'Claughtons' had been rebuilt with larger boilers and a working pressure of 200lb sq in instead of 175; but at the times I was travelling they were rarely to be seen around London. The 10 fitted with Caprotti valve-gear were mostly divided between Holyhead and Longsight sheds. The former worked regularly on the double-home turns instituted not long previously on the 'Irish Mails' between Holyhead and Euston. These employed four of the Caprotti engines daily. I discovered later that the rebuilds with Walschaerts valve gear were mostly concentrated on Preston, for working the Liverpool and Manchester Scotch express to and from Carlisle. In the autumn of 1930 an event that rather shocked me, as a strong North Western supporter, was the drastic rebuilding of two of the 'Claughtons' with three cylinders — actually the first two of the well-known 'Baby Scot' class. Their allocation to the Midland Division attracted my attention once again to that line, and I used to cycle over from Bushey to Radlett to watch and photograph the trains.

At that time the express passenger service was almost exclusively worked by compounds, with only an occasional Class 2 or Class 3 turning up on a semi-fast. The freights were much more interesting. The LMS had brought out the Midlandised version of the LNWR superheater 0-8-0 and a number of these were working on the lighter goods trains from Cricklewood. The old, invariably double-headed combinations of a 2 and a 4, or a 1 and a 4 had disappeared; but on the heaviest mineral trains the Garratts were used. These had the nominal tractive power of two Class 3 engines, having $18\frac{1}{2}$in by 26in cylinders, and with the typically puissant Garratt boiler they eliminated double heading on the freight trains of the Midland Division. They were most spectacular things to see in action. My only grouse about them was that they usually worked cab first in the up direction when they were pulling a maximum load and likely to give an impressive exhaust.

The change in family circumstances brought a change in my travelling. With no occasion to go to Barrow at holiday weekends I began to plan other expeditions, and an early one took me to Penrith as a base for some photography on Shap and mountain walking in the Lake District. It was then that I saw the rebuilt 'Claughtons' having the Walschaerts valve gear in action. Six out of the 10 engines of this group were stationed at Preston, in 1931, and the shed staff kept them. most regally clean. For the record the six engines thus allocated were Nos 5906 *Ralph Brocklebank*, 5910 *J. A. Bright*, 5953 *Buckingham*, 5970 *Patience*, and two unnamed ones, Nos 5986 and 5993. On that first trip I went up by a night train, and was out early next morning to see them coming through. As a spectacle in the Shap area they completely stole the show; but I saw also that they were going well, with heavy trains, and for my next visits I arranged my travelling to include some runs on the Liverpool and Manchester trains to Carlisle. While their performance was not up to the amazing heights set by the original 'Claughtons' in their prime it was certainly very good, and I never saw one of them need to take a pilot over Shap. The heaviest load I saw one of them take was 393 tons tare, 415 tons full. This was with No 5906 *Ralph Brocklebank*. The train was on time from the start; we kept time almost to the second to Shap Summit, afterwards running fast down to Carlisle.

On one of my earliest weekend trips to this area, for my return run south I went to Carlisle prepared to take the first train that looked interesting. The 'Royal Scot' itself was evidently very heavy, because coupled to the engine that was to take it nominally non-stop to Euston, was a 2P standard 4-4-0. There was a rebuilt 'Claughton' waiting for the Liverpool and Manchester train, and one of the first two 'Baby Scots', No 5971, waiting for the Thames-Clyde Express, to St Pancras. I decided for the last mentioned, but was disappointed in getting no more than a moderate load of 290 tons. The performance was very dull and unenterprising; in fact, by far the most interesting work was done south of Leeds, by compounds No 1059 to Leicester, and No 1102 onwards. I went Midland again at August

Bank Holiday, and got some excellent runs with unrebuilt 'Claughtons' between Leeds and Carlisle. One of these featured *Sir Gilbert Claughton* itself, on which the cleaners had done a job almost to outshine even the most brilliant of the Preston 5Xs. On the last stage of my run south I had a particularly good run from Leicester to St Pancras behind one of the original Johnson compounds, No 1003 (originally No 2634) but in 1931 of course rebuilt to conform to the standard superheated Fowler type.

During visits to the Carlisle area I took the opportunity of going to Kingmoor shed, which in the early 1930s was still strongly Caledonian in its aspects. Sunday morning is usually a good time for finding plenty of engines on shed, and on one such visit I had a photographic field day. There were, for example, two out of the four Pickersgill 3-cylinder 4-6-0s outside, one of them, significantly perhaps, with a front cylinder cover removed and part of the motion dismantled. Those four engines remain today the most inexplicable 'flops' in British locomotive history. They were supremely beautiful to look at, glorious in their original 'Caledonian blue' yet about the most useless engines that ever ran the road, in Great Britain, or anywhere else one would imagine. The reputation of William Pickersgill as an engine designer is one of the great enigmas of all time. He was a scholarly man, a charming personality, and he inherited from John F. McIntosh a design, construction and running organisation that had attained a towering reputation . It would perhaps be unkind to suggest that the four new classes of main line engine that he introduced let the Caledonian side down; but his record at St Rollox is really difficult to explain. Some day one hopes that a truly erudite historian will elucidate the period.

There was no particular puzzle surrounding the 60 class 2-cylinder 4-6-0s, of which there were usually a number on shed at Kingmoor. They were a massive very handsome design; but in the machinery Pickersgill put in Stephenson's link motion with *crossed* instead of open eccentric rods. This meant that the inherent characteristic of the link motion, the variation in lead as the engine was linked up, was reversed from the normal. The 60 class had maximum lead in full gear, when they did not need it, and minimum when they were fully linked up to their running position. The result was that they were weaker than their dimensions promised when starting away, and hamstrung for lack of lead when running at such speed as they could make on the level or downhill. I made a number of runs with them, chiefly north of Glasgow, and found them painfully sluggish. But why, oh why, were those eccentric rods crossed?

The 4-4-0s were strong, massively built and trouble-free engines, but in speed and maximum output they could not hold a candle to the superheated 'Dunalastair IV' class introduced in McIntosh's time. The huge query that hangs over these two designs is how the experienced men of the St Rollox drawing office were persuaded to finalise these designs as they were. The Oban 4-6-0s and the 3-cylinder 956 class were essentially new designs, and both very bad ones. The Oben engines, as I found later from the footplate could not produce enough steam to supply their cylinders in any instance of hard work, and they were non-superheated into the bargain — a bargain that is of a negative kind. On the 956 class Pickersgill had a form of conjugated valve gear for actuating the valves of the inside cylinder. It was a device very much more complicated than the Gresley gear which Pickersgill once euphemistically described as 'a wee contraption of m'own'! To try to make something of these beautiful looking engines, two out of the four were fitted with separate Stephenson's link motion for the inside cylinder, but to no avail.

On Kingmoor shed that same day I found one of Peter Drummond's big 2-6-0 express goods engines, one of the longest lived classes of all Glasgow and South Western design. Of the 11 engines of the class originally built by the North British Locomotive Company in 1915 10 went to Carlisle from the outset, and remained there for many years. The G&SWR sheds at Carlisle were somewhat occult from popular gaze, at any rate from passengers on the principal main lines. I remember F. E. Mackay telling me how, before World War I, he spent a whole afternoon walking around Carlisle to try and find them. They were tucked away at Currock Road, beside the Maryport and Carlisle line, and the enginemen for the most part were broadspoken Cumbrians. The shed was closed after Grouping and to the disgust of all Sou' West men the engines were moved to Kingmoor. But those superheated Drummond 2-6-0s were splendid engines, of a quality that even Caledonian prejudice could not ignore, and the last of them was not scrapped until 1947. This was the very engine I photographed at Kingmoor, No 17829, standing at the head of a line-up, followed by a Caledonian 2-6-0, a 3-cylinder 956 class, and a Pickersgill 60 class.

The big inside-cylinder Caledonian 4-6-0s of McIntosh design were much in evidence at Perth shed at this particular time, though I was too late to see the 'Cardeans' in their last years. The mixed traffic types of the 'Barochan' class and the still larger class with side-windowed cabs and numbered by the LMS from No 17905 upwards were being used on passenger and goods trains alike. In 1929 I had found No 14609, one of the 'Barochans', still in red, with her number in large numerals on the tender, acting as station pilot at Aberdeen. One of my most interesting captures with the camera in 1931-2 was the Caledonian 4-2-2 No 123, in her last years as a regular traffic engine. Stationed at Perth she was then painted black, numbered 14010, and working local trains between Perth and Dundee. She was reasonably clean, but not very attractive looking in plain black.

In the early 1930s it was a real bonus activity in one's railway interests to have such a proliferation of ex-LNWR engine classes, not only on the doorstep, as it were but concerned in my daily travelling to and from business. I have already mentioned the 8.53am from Watford Junction to Euston. This was exclusively a superheater engine working; but in the evening we had a Euston to Bushey non-stop at 6.15pm on which the motive power was anything from non-superheated 'Precursors' and 'Experiments' upwards. It was a 7-coach train of 215 tons, and the 'Experiments' used to fairly sail up Camden bank, though the superheated 'Precursors' and 'Princes' would overtake them afterwards. I have notes of the following 'Experiments' on the job in 1931; *Buffalo*, *City of Edinburgh*, *Herefordshire*, *John Penn*; *President*; *Sarmatian*; *Sisyphus*. Curiously enough one of the poorest runs I had on that evening train, was an unusual night when one of the Horwich 'Moguls' was put on. She made a bad start up Camden bank and ran feebly afterwards. It was however our morning 'flyer' that provided the thrills, and in those years of the Great Slump the railways were doing a considerable amount of advertising to try and win back traffic that had been lost to the roads. I remember a perversion of the famous Scottish ballad ran thus:

'Ye'll take the high road,
'And I'll take the rail road,
'And I'll be in Scotland afore ye . . .'

A further perversion might have been applied to our morning services from Bushey to Euston, because there were two electric trains that ran from Bushey at almost the same time, one up and one down. By taking the latter to Watford Junction one could catch the 8.53am up non-stop. The rhyme could then be adapted:

'Ye'll take the UP road
'And I'll take the DOWN road
'And I'll be in Euston afore ye!'

... because the respective arrivals were 9.14am steam and 9.18am electric!

One Saturday in March 1932 however I went the other way from Watford Junction, on a trip to Rugby, via Northampton. I was hoping that some old engines might be around, working on the branch trains, and I was lucky enough to find one of the very last of the LNWR 2-4-0 'Jumbos' to remain in revenue earning service, No 5018 *Talavera*. At that time there were only 12 of them left, several of which were stationed at Rugby. *Talavera* carried the date 1868 on her nameplates, though that was the date of the Ramsbottom 'Newton' class 2-4-0 No 1672, which like the other 95 engines of that class had been renewed by F. W. Webb as 'Precedents' by 1894. I was delighted to find that *Talavera* was booked to take the 3.30pm local express to Rugby, and although that train consisted of no more than three coaches it was pleasant to ride behind a 'Jumbo' working solo, in that year of grace. She accelerated to 50mph up the long rise at 1 in 230 from Northampton up past Long Buckby, passing the summit point $12\frac{1}{4}$ miles in $17\frac{3}{4}$ min. After that came an easy downhill run into Rugby.

The appointment of W. A. Stanier as Chief Mechanical Engineer of the LMS, as from January 1932, caused many speculations, and I remember Mac Pearson writing to me and suggesting that before long we would have 'Flowers' in crimson working the 6.15pm 'Bushey Flyer' at nights! I have however very special reasons to remember the introduction of the first Pacific in 1933. I had been successful in interesting one of the features editors of *The Star* in short chatty railway articles, and after the new engines had settled down to their appointed duties, working through over the 401 miles between Euston and Glasgow he agreed that an article describing one such run, from the footplate, would be a possibility. It was by no means a definite commission, but it was enough to embolden me to ask for a footplate pass. I had by that time contributed a number of articles to *The Railway Magazine* and apparently my work, and the runs of mine that had been used in Cecil J. Allen's articles had not been unnoticed at Euston, and I was readily given permission to ride both ways, if I so wished.

I shall never forget that Easter of 1934. The LMS were anxious to get some additional publicity for the new engines, because they had not been proving particularly reliable, and were frequently unable to work their scheduled rosters, one each way daily on the 'Royal Scot' train throughout between Euston and Glasgow. A week before I was due to make my trips D. S. Barrie, then a senior assistant in the Publicity Department at Euston, telephoned to say that neither of the 'Pacifics' was in service, but that they hoped one at least would be available for the Easter week-end. When I travelled up to London early on the Saturday morning sure enough No 6201 was on the shed; but I also saw a 'Scot', No 6137, then named *Vesta* with her tender piled with coal to the limit of the loading gauge, and obviously the prepared engine for the Carlisle run. A 'Royal Scot' was a scarifying engine on which to make a first main line express passenger footplate trip, particularly in that the tender was considerably narrower than the engine cab, and that from the fireman's seat, to which I was ushered, one looked back into an airy nothing! On the other hand I could not have had more delightful companions than Driver Charlton and Fireman Baker, of Upperby shed, Carlisle. This is saying something, after all the thousands of miles I have ridden on locomotives, all over the world, but I do not think I have ever been made more welcome, or to feel more of an honoured guest than I was on No 6137.

In the mid-1930s the 'Scots', with their piston valves changed to have solid heads and six narrow rings, and with Stanier's modification to their driving axle boxes, were touching absolutely top form, and some of the runs I logged with the top link men at Camden, Crewe North and Carlisle sheds were, I must admit, finer than anything that came to my personal notice with the 'Converted Scots' in British Railways days. The working of the 'Royal Scot' train, with one engine over the 299.2 miles between Euston and Carlisle was a severe assignment, but with an engine like No 6137 and men like Charlton and Baker it was made to look easy, and experiencing it on the footplate threw into more striking contrast the struggle I witnessed three days later, returning non-stop from Carlisle to Euston on the first of the 'Pacifics', No 6200 *The Princess Royal*. Incidentally, at that time the LMS did not like them referred to as Pacifics in case they were confused, by an untutored public, with the Gresley Pacifics of the LNER. That run of mine on No 6200, with a load of 500 tons, was a continual struggle for steam, and anything but complimentary to the design. Had we not had a driver of the energy, enthusiasm and determination of Laurie Earl, we should almost certainly have had to stop, once at least, for a 'blow up'.

Of course all this had to be not only glossed over, but completely concealed in the article I wrote for *The Star*. Fortunately, due to Earl's work, we finished 4min early into Euston, and this apparent triumph sounded the keynote of the article as it eventually appeared. My first draft did not have enough human touches for them. I added many more, and then a sub-editor prefaced the piece with a very flowery and journalesey opening. I was rather horrified when I saw this, because Euston House was rather touchy about approval of scripts, and this had been added after they had vetted my final draft. But all was well; Barrie telephoned me to say that everyone was pleased with the results of the privileges they had given me, and the experience turned out to be a big breakthrough for me, and the first of an increasing number of footplate passes I was given, not only on the LMS, but elsewhere.

The flowery accord given to this run did not finish with *The Star*. Naturally I sent a copy of the full log with some details of the engine working to Cecil J. Allen for possible use in the 'British Locomotive Practice and Performance' feature in *The Railway Magazine*. He swooped upon it with relish, and worked it up into a tribute that was not really justified by the facts. At the request of Euston House I had avoided all reference to the great difficulty we had in maintaining anything in the way of steam pressure and to the labour of keeping that large grate adequately fed; and so while telling Allen of the regulator and cut-off position I made no reference at all to the boiler pressure. Fortunately from the viewpoint of pro-LMS publicity he did not detect from the figures I gave him that anything had been wrong. His article was indeed another tremendous boost for the design.

Concerning especially the work south of Crewe he wrote: 'Performance grew steadily finer as London was neared and culminated in the time of 65min 33sec for the 72.9 miles from Welton to South Hampstead, an average of 66.7mph, which included the excellent time of 15min 12sec from Bletchley up to Tring.' If only he had known! For a solid two hours, from Whitmore to Tring, it was touch and go whether the fire could be replenished. Fortunately the engine needed no driving in the ordinary sense; the cut-off was kept at 20% throughout, and the only movement of the regulator from the full open position was in observing the speed restrictions at Stafford, Polesworth and Rugby. The coal was not trimming forward from the back of the tender, and Earl spent a good deal of his time from Stafford southwards shovelling supplies forward. It was a curious three man team on that engine: the driver up in the tender getting coal forward; the fireman piling it in for all he was worth, and their visitor keenly scanning the road ahead for the first sight of any adverse signal. Fortunately there were none. Boiler pressure was often below 200lb sq in instead of 250; the injectors were shut off occasionally to help rally the pressure, while the process of coal heaving by these *two* heroes went on. Performance growing finer indeed! We struggled up to Tring with pressure down to 200, and the water down 2in in the gauge glasses, and once over Tring and a slight relaxing of the firing, the needle dropped back to 165. But no one in that long train could have been any the wiser; and on arrival at Euston all there was to show for it was a tender practically empty of coal, three very black faces, and an arrival 4min early.

How Stanier and his men profited from the gruelling experiences with the first two Pacifics — sorry, Euston House, 4-6-2s! — and produced magnificent engines is a later story; but here I must add that other new designs of the Stanier regime did not get away to a very good start either. During the summer and autumn of 1934 most of my travelling to and from the north was on the eastern side of the country, and it was not until 1935 that I had my first runs with the 'Black five' 4-6-0s and with the 'Jubilees'. One of the former, No 5153 did well one Sunday morning with the up Ulster Express, from Lancaster down to Crewe, with a heavy train of 490 tons, but the 'Jubilees' were not impressive. One Saturday evening in the late autumn I went down from St Pancras to Leeds prior to some signalling changeover work, and a 'Jubilee' made a very poor show with with an 8-coach train with which any self-respecting Midland compound would have made light work. I had a talk with the driver on arrival and he was scathing in his comments: 'Superheaters' he snorted, 'the things they have on these engines wouldn't heat water, let alone steam! It is, of course, well known nowadays that once Great Western ideas on superheating had been discarded the 'Jubilees' became great engines. In later years I had some tremendous runs with them, even during the worst war conditions.

Top: Elimination of double-heading on the Midland mineral trains; a 2-6-0 + 0-6-2 Beyer-Garratt No 4987 on loaded coal train for Cricklewood, approaching Radlett.

Above: Liverpool and Mancester Scottish express climbing Shap, hauled by large boilered 'Claughton' class 4-6-0 No 5993 (piston valve type).

Below: A famous name on the West Coast route: *Charles Dickens*, on the 'George the Fifth' class 4-4-0 No 5380 (LNWR No 82) at Willesden shed. At the time this engine was stationed at Edge Hill.

Above: Watford Junction sheds in 1931, showing a 0-6-2 suburban tank No 6872; an 18-inch 0-6-0 goods ('Cauliflower') No 8442, a Webb non-compound 0-8-0 No 8976, and a 'Precursor' 4-4-2T — all ex-LNWR types.

Above centre left: The Engineer's Department private engine at Watford. This was originally one of the 'Whitworth', or 6ft 'Jumbo' series No 793 *Martin* built at Crewe in May 1894 in replacement of a 'Samson' class 2-4-0 of the same name and number. It was transferred to the Engineer's Department in 1923.

Below centre left: Up main line goods passing Watford Tunnel north signalbox, hauled by one of the Horwich type 2-6-0s (Crabs) No 13081, at the time painted red. The characteristic LNWR semaphore signals are much in evidence in this picture.

Below: Webb 0-8-0 No 8976 on ballast train at Bushey troughs — Sunday occupation. This engine was originally a 3-cylinder compound, but it was rebuilt with two $18\frac{1}{2}$in diameter cylinders.

Top: An ex-LNWR 'Precursor Tank' 4-4-2T, used on the London residential services, here seen at Watford Junction.

Above: One of the new LMS 2-6-4Ts that replaced the LNWR 4-4-2Ts, and which made exceptionally fast running on the Euston commuter services.

Below: One of the LMS 0-8-0 freight engines developed from the ex-LNWR G2 class here seen working a train of the special coal hoppers used for supplies to Stonebridge Park power station. This train of empties is approaching Bushey.

Above: LMS standard 3-cylinder compound No 1122, on station pilot duty at Rugby.

Below: The down 'Royal Scot', climbing Shap, hauled by engine No 6160, in original condition before the smoke-deflecting plates were added. This photograph was taken at Whitsun 1931 when a westerly gale was sweeping across the moor.

Bottom: Beginning of the new order at Euston: the second of the Stanier Pacifics, No 6201 *Princess Elizabeth* in No 2 platform, having brought in the 'Royal Scot'. The engine has worked through from Glasgow and carries the Caledonian type route indicator. Alongside is a 'Baby Scot' No 6015 that has brought in a Manchester express.

9
Footplating on the Southern

By the beginning of the 1930s the pundits generally felt that steam was on its way out on the Southern. The General Manager, Sir Herbert Walker, was a strong advocate of electrification; the second stage of conversion of the Brighton line was completed in time for electric trains to begin running as far south as Three Bridges from July 1932, and but for the world-wide depression, which severely curtailed schemes involving high capital expenditure work would already have commenced on further electrification projects. The whole of Kent, the Portsmouth lines, and that to Southampton and Bournemouth were all marked down for conversion, and steam men in their moments of depression felt that the only thing to be done with what was left, west of Basingstoke, was to hand it over to the Great Western!

To make things worse, the prestige of steam traction then did not stand very high on the Southern. In 1926 the *Lord Nelson* had come out to a mighty blast of trumpets from the publicity department at Waterloo, as the most powerful express locomotive in Great Britain. So it was on the basis of nominal tractive effort; but even though that claim was handsomely surpassed, on the same basis, a year later, by the introduction of the 'King' class on the Great Western, if it had come to scientifically controlled interchange trials the 'Nelsons' would have been very hard put to it to equal the daily work of the Gresley 'Super-Pacifics' of the LNER or that of the 'Royal Scots' with the improved piston valves. So, it had not been surprising that connoisseurs of locomotive working whose enthusiasms lay elsewhere cocked a rather cynical eye towards the introduction of another Southern steam design, which on tractive effort basis was claimed as the most powerful of its kind — the most powerful 4-4-0 in Europe, in fact.

In view of the general policy towards electrification it would have seemed that the Southern was amply furnished with reasonably up-to-date steam power at the end of the 1920s, with 74 express 4-6-0s of the N15 class and 16 Nelsons. But the structural clearances on the Hastings Line precluded the use of the large 4-6-0s, and because some improvement of service was desired a request was made to R. E. L. Maunsell for a more powerful type of locomotive than the L1 class 4-4-0s. The small headquarters staff of the CME, at Waterloo, prepared an ingenious compromise, using a maximum of standard parts that would minimise the capital cost of construction. Thus, with a shortened version of the 'King Arthur' boiler, using all its flanging plates and so on, and cylinders and motion similar to that of the 'Nelson', but three instead of four, a powerful 4-4-0 was evolved that would comply with all the structural restrictions of the Hastings line and have a nominal tractive effort practically equal to the 6-coupled 'King Arthur'.

When the 'Schools' class first came out in 1930 and their assignation to the Hastings line was announced, it was inferred that although apparently somewhat over-cylindered in relation to their boiler capacity this would not matter, because the demands for steam on that hilly road would be no more than intermittent. An examination of the size and disposition of the tubes in the 'King Arthur' and 'Schools' boilers showed that the reduced distance between tube plates on the 4-4-0 had encouraged the designer to use a smaller diameter of tube, namely $1\frac{3}{4}$in outside, and 216 of them, against the 2in tubes of the 'King Arthur' and only 167. The heating surface contributed by the small tubes was practically the same, 1,205sq ft 'Schools' against 1,252 'King Arthur'. The shorter barrel resulted in a reduced heating surface in the superheaters, both designs having 24 elements. It so happened however that the civil engineer had not completed alterations on the Hastings line that would allow the 'Schools' to run, and for the first months of their existence they were stationed at Deal. The former SE&CR shed there was then responsible for working the Folkestone and Dover expresses, before the alterations in Thanet were completed, and Ramsgate became the principal locomotive depot.

That brief sojourn of the first 10 'Schools' class engines at Deal however showed them in a guise that had not been expected — as capable of a sustained high power performance virtually equal to that of the 'King Arthurs'. It was indeed a year before they were transferred to St Leonards shed to take up the work for which they had been designed. I timed some runs with them between Cannon Street and Tunbridge Wells in the late autumn of 1931, but was not impressed. Making allowance for loads, the old L class SE&CR 4-4-0s of 1914 seemed to do as well, if not better. It was not until some professional work began to take me down to Dover from time to time, and I logged the 80min Folkestone expresses that I realised that here was an outstanding locomotive, that fully justified its claim to be the most powerful 4-4-0 in Europe. Having obtained the entrée to the footplate on the LMS, as described in the previous chapter, I began to think round how I could approach the Southern for similar facilities. The trouble was that the railways of Britain in seeking means of publicity did not regard the technical or semi-technical journals as worth their while. As one PRO expressed it, in *The Railway Magazine* one is 'preaching to the converted'. They wanted to get through to the general public, and it was with that article in *The Star* that I had made my breakthrough with the LMS. How was I to do it on the Southern? So far as the daily newspapers were concerned there was nothing new about the 'Schools' in 1934; but then an opportunity came at the opposite end of the line.

I cannot remember now just what topical peg I hung on it, but having established contact with Wilson Midgley, features editor of *The Star*, through my piece on *The Princess Royal* I managed to interest him in a 'story' of the express meat train that left Exeter each evening, and brought up a heavy load for the early morning Smithfield Market. The Southern obliged readily enough with a footplate pass, and I rode first an S15 4-6-0 to Salisbury, and then a 'King Arthur' into Nine Elms goods station. It did not yield any very exciting work from the locomotive performance viewpoint. I thought the 'King Arthur', No 778 *Sir Pelleas* was very much run down, from the roughness and vibration of the going; though subsequent experiences in other engines of the class, in later years showed that this particular engine as not much out of the ordinary. *The Star* duly 'splashed' the article; the Southern were pleased, and the ice was duly broken for me.

It was then, or just after, that another approach opened up. I had been contributing occasional short articles to *The Meccano Magazine*, and the point was put to me that while writing for *The Railway Magazine* was at that time regarded as 'preaching to the converted' *The Meccano Magazine* directed towards boys who were taking an intelligent interest in all matters mechanical, could well be an organ of pro-railway propaganda among teenagers. With that magazine primarily in view the Southern gave me footplate passes for a trip to Dover and back on 'Schools' class engines. Through my journeys thence for other purposes I had already amassed quite a collection of runs, including many on the 5.10pm up from Folkestone, and had built up a general assessment of the working; but as sometimes happens when one goes to make a special observation the circumstances are initially less interesting that one would have hoped. Going down on Saturdays, by the 12.55pm from Charing Cross prior to weekend work on the line I had sometimes noted loads of 12 coaches, up to 410 tons; but on the day for my footplate run we had the minimum load for that train of nine coaches.

The techniques used by different drivers on the 'Schools' interested me very much, because there seemed no standard, no generally recognised way of handling them. The one thing that seemed to be common was to take them very gently away from rest. One could understand this in starting away from Charing Cross, or Waterloo Junction, where cautious running was in any case necessary for the first mile or so; but it was the same when starting west bound from Folkestone, with sharp point to point bookings. On reflection, of course, handling them gently at the start was logical enough, seeing that with the same nominal tractive effort they had only two-thirds of the adhesion weight of a 'King Arthur'. Most drivers worked them with a relatively narrow regulator opening and in cut-offs of 25 to 30%, and in such conditions they simply flew along with the loads of around 300 to 330 tons. They were very light on coal, and were generally very popular with their crews. I did however ride with one Ramsgate driver who worked his engine with a wide open regulator and short cut-offs. It did not seem to make any difference either to the economy, or the running of the machine. The action was just as smooth and effortless.

The draft of my article for *The Meccano Magazine* was passed without comment at Waterloo, but as usual I prepared fully detailed logs, with particulars of the engine working, boiler pressures and so on, for eventual use in *The Railway Magazine*. I enjoyed the close friendship of W. A. Willox, then Associate Editor of *The Railway Gazette* as well as being Editor of *The Railway Magazine*, and on one of my visits to his office I took the logs. He asked me if I knew A. B. MacLeod. The name had been familiar to me for many years from his photographs and occasional contributions to the railway press. Willox suggested I should meet him, because he was then Assistant Running Superintendent of the Southern Railway, and as Willox emphasised, an enthusiast of the first water. His chief was then A. Cobb, on whose authority my footplate passes had been issued, though as one outside the railway service my application had been made through the Public Relations department.

Through Willox's introduction an appointment was arranged for me with MacLeod, and it proved the beginning of a lifelong friendship. I took the details of my Folkestone runs to show him, and he thought that Cobb should see them too. He asked me to send them in officially, but added: 'I'll see he *does* see them'. This last remark was no surprise to me, from my increasing knowledge of official business. A letter might be addressed to a chief officer, but some subordinate through whom correspondence passed upward, might, to avoid 'bothering' the chief, send a formal acknowledgement and consign the letter to the files, or the dustbin. In that very pleasant first conversation I had with MacLeod he suggested that I might find the faster Portsmouth trains even more interesting, and that if I cared to apply for engine passes he would pave the way for their issue. It was important therefore that Cobb saw the very detailed records I had made of the Folkestone runs. It was also essential that I made the runs fairly soon because of the impending electrification of the Portsmouth direct line, via Petersfield. He told me also that it was the intention to move the 10 'Schools' class engines then stationed at Fratton to Bournemouth when the electric service on the Portsmouth line began.

This last was surprising news to me. While the 'Schools' class engines had done very well on the Folkestone expresses the loads were considerably lighter than those on the Bournemouth route, and above all there was more give and take about the gradient profile. One always thought about boiler capacity in relation to tractive effort where the 'Schools' were concerned, and on the down run from Waterloo there was absolutely no let-up in the first 56 miles. With trains loading regularly to over 400 tons, and requiring the summit point at Litchfield to be passed in about 63 or 64min, this would be a pretty gruelling test for a 4-4-0 engine of whatever capacity. However my immediate concern were the 90min Portsmouth expresses. This again was a hard road, but hard in a different way. After going out to Byfleet in the style of the best Bournemouth expresses there came the very difficult central part of the run, from Woking to Havant, 42 miles booked in $52\frac{1}{2}$min, beset with speed restrictions, and the gruelling climb at 1 in 80 up to Haslemere. Altogether, to do the 73.6 miles from Waterloo to Portsmouth in 90min, although involving an average speed of no more than 49.2mph start to stop, was a tough proposition with train loads up to 11 of the latest coaches, about 360 tons tare.

At the same time, the incidence of speed restrictions of the severity of those at Woking and Guildford, involved a break in the steaming, and can provide a brief though welcome respite if the boiler pressure in tending to droop. Furthermore, once over the summit at Haslemere there is a glorious racing stretch down through Liss and Petersfield that enables the ascent to Buriton Tunnel to be rushed. There were no permanent speed restrictions on this length, and the 'Schools' could be allowed to *run*. Because of my daily work at that time I had to make footplate journeys at the weekend; while this gave me heavier loads it often involved checks from congestion on the line. The 11.50am down 90min express to Portsmouth was a case in point. It was at the end of June, and holiday traffic to Southsea and the Isle of Wight was building up to summer intensity. The convergence of the former Brighton and South Western lines at Havant tended to saturate the section west of that junction; and while the timetabling was skilfully arranged to provide for any extra trains, and for the disposal of their carriages and engines from the somewhat limited track facilities at Portsmouth and Southsea (High Level) and at Portsmouth Harbour, it did not need much in the way of late running by one or more of the preceding trains to create a major snarl-up, as road traffic people would call it.

On engine No 924 *Haileybury* I enjoyed a splendid run down from Waterloo, with a 10-coach train of 350 tons, gross, behind the tender. Despite two checks for permanent way repairs — one between Liphook and Liss that was very long and down to 15mph — we passed Havant practically on time, in $81\frac{1}{4}$min for the 66.4 miles from Waterloo. Our driver, May of Fratton, was most apologetic about the Liss check. 'Pity about this', he said, 'I could have shown you how she'd go'. As we were already doing 74mph on the slightly falling stretch south of Liphook *before* coming on to the 2 miles of 1 in 80 down to Liss, I imagine that we should have got very near to a full 90mph at the foot of this beautifully aligned road, instead of creeping funereally down it at 15mph. This driver had the services of a splendid fireman named Mintram, who sad to say was killed while serving in the Royal Navy, in World War II. The driver handled the engine skilfully, working mostly between 26 and 30%, cut-off, with fairly frequent changes in the regulator position to suit the sharp alterations of adverse and favourable gradients, but the most interesting work was on the severe climb to Haslemere, begun from the severe speed restriction through Guildford. On the gently rising approach, speed was worked up to 59mph through Godalming, after which it gradually fell to a minimum of 26mph on the final ascent at 1 in 80.

Passing Havant in such good time, having recovered the time lost from the two slacks we seemed in good form for a punctual finish. With a quick recovery on the level of the coast line we were past Farlington Junction in $84\frac{3}{4}$min, at 60mph with only 4 miles left to go; but then we struck it. The Portsmouth area was blocked solid with holiday trains, just queueing up to get down to the Harbour station, and believe it or not that last 4 miles took us *twenty nine minutes*. But the trip had given me another excellent example of the working of the 'Schools' class locomotives. So far as steaming was concerned, the pressure gauge needle was so consistently near to the red line that I did not need to log its minute variations. There was no 90min express back to London on that afternoon, so I spent a pleasant two hours photographing, stayed the night in Portsmouth and footplated the 10.16am up to Waterloo on the Sunday morning.

Summer Saturdays could be the photographer's Valhalla, on the Southern. All shapes and vintages of engines made their way down to Portsmouth Harbour, but I was particularly interested in the working of the Drummond D15 4-4-0s, which as I told in Chapter Two at one time had something of a monopoly of the Waterloo-Bournemouth service. On the Waterloo-Portsmouth run, in 1936-7, they were playing the part of 'understudy' to the 'Schools', but in so doing, because of the reduced length of run they had relatively small 6-wheeled tenders in place of the big 8-wheeled Drummond 'watercarts'. Naturally their performance was not up to that of the 'Schools', but they did very good work with the intermediate express trains. I travelled behind No 465 on the 5.25 up from Haslemere one afternoon, and on the non-stop run of 30.3 miles from Guildford to Waterloo her running was fully up to the standard required on the 90min Portsmouth non-stops. This was with a gross load behind the tender of 310 tons.

My return footplate trip on the 10.16am Sunday train was a most exciting experience, with engine No 925 *Cheltenham*, and a gross load of 395 tons (11 coaches packed). We got a bad start along the coast, signals checking us all the way to Havant, which we passed $4\frac{1}{2}$min late; but we climbed well to Buriton, went like the wind down through Petersfield, touching $83\frac{1}{2}$mph and went magnificently up to Haslemere. We were then only $1\frac{1}{2}$min late; but we suffered two permanent way checks on the descent to Guildford, and in consequence passed Woking and entered on to the main line 2min late. Some very fast running followed, touching $77\frac{1}{2}$mph on the very slight descent before Esher, and when we passed Surbiton, 12 miles short of Waterloo, with 14min left I thought that perhaps even with the delays we had experienced so far we might just scrape in on time. But it was not to be. There was another permanent way check at Malden, and right at the finish we were brought almost to a stop at Vauxhall. So, our eventual time was 94min, though the delays we had experienced accounted for a full 12min in running. This left a net time of 82min from Portsmouth, and a very fine overall average speed of 54mph.

The transfer of the 10 'Schools' class engines from Fratton to Bournemouth shed was followed by one of the most remarkable transformations in British motive power history. The top link drivers at Bournemouth had not been among the more enterprising of Southern links. This tradition indeed went back to London and South Western days. When they had the Drummond 4-4-0s, and then the 'King Arthurs' one could record any amount of steady reliable work, but never the brilliant feats of time recovery that sometimes came with the enginemen of Nine Elms, Salisbury and Exmouth Junction. But when they got the 'Schools' there was an almost unbelievable change, and some of the work done in the last years before World War II was outstanding to the last degree. On the trains booked to cover the 108 miles between Waterloo and Bournemouth Central in the level two hours the loads were limited to 11 coaches, about 350 tons tare, and with this limitation I have known time kept despite 8min delay en route. But on the ordinary expresses stopping intermediately at Southampton, and then requiring the 79.3 miles from Waterloo to be covered in 87min there seemed no load that the Bournemouth drivers were not prepared to take with those marvellous little 4-4-0 engines, and to have some time in hand. I have known loads of up to 250 tons worked down to Southampton on time.

One naturally searches round for an explanation. I think it lies in the way the 'Schools' class engines responded to working on a light rein. One never needed to thrash them. On that exciting trip of mine up from Portsmouth *Cheltenham* was worked on a cut-off of 29% unchanged from start to finish, and never more than the first part of the regulator. From the footplate she never seemed, or sounded as if she was working hard; and I could quite imagine that the Bournemouth drivers, who had such a tradition for quiet and effortless running with 'King Arthurs' naturally adopted methods that ideally suited the 'Schools'. In actual fact however, with their quiet 3-cylinder exhaust and low coal consumption they would have been working a good deal harder than their drivers realised! They steamed very freely and gave their firemen no trouble. The one thing I regret above all with the 'Schools' is that they were never put through a series of full-dress thermodynamic trials on one or other of the stationary testing plants. They were undoubtedly one of the most remarkable engine classes that ever ran the road in Great Britain, and it would have been good to have an exhaustive analysis of their performance.

In the course of my travelling around the various sections of the Southern Railway in those later years between the wars, with many fine runs with 'King Arthurs' to add to those of the 'Schools', there was one locomotive class to which I was particularly attracted, more for sentimental reasons than any other. As a boy I had seen the huge Drummond T14 4-cylinder 4-6-0s racing through Basingstoke with West of England expresses, and although they had been much modified by the years 1936-7 they still retained some of their old characteristics — not however their huge coupled wheel splashers, which gave rise to their nickname of the 'Paddle-boats'. Then one day in July 1939 I had occasion to go down to Bournemouth, and found No 443, the first of the class on the 11.22am relief, with a load of 315 tons. No 'Schools', 'Arthur', or 'Nelson' could attract me away from taking this train, and old 443 gave me a splendid run down to Southampton. She made good time on the long upward pull to Basingstoke, followed by a merry dash down past Winchester, touching 82mph. It was the last down run I had on the Southern before World War II and it remains a happy memory.

Top left: Southern Railway, the 'Atlantic Coast Express' approaching Honiton Tunnel. The locomotive, 'King Arthur' class 4-6-0 No 768 *Sir Balin*, has a straight sided 8-wheeled tender as used on some of the 'Lord Nelson' class locomotives.

Above left: 'Schools' class 4-4-0 No 912 *Downside*, on Ramsgate express at Dover Priory.

Left: Hastings express entering Crowhurst, hauled by 'Schools' class 4-4-0 No 911 *Dover*.

Top: Ramsgate-Charing Cross express, via Dover, leaving Folkestone Central, hauled by 'Schools' class 4-4-0 No 916 *Whitgift*.

Above: 'Schools' class 4-4-0 No 931 *Kings Wimbledon* on Portsmouth express at Waterloo.

Top: The most distinguished of the Drummond T9 class 4-4-0s, No 119, — an engine frequently requisitioned for Royal Train workings on the Southern, here seen at Portsmouth Harbour.

Centre: One of the 90min Waterloo-Portsmouth expresses topping the steep gradient on the crest of the North Downs near Haslemere. The locomotive is 'Schools' class 4-4-0 No 930 *Radley.*

Above: Engines of down expresses at Waterloo: on left 'Urie-Arthur' 4-6-0 No 750 *Morgan le Fay* and on right one of Drummond 'Paddleboats' as rebuilt, No 458. This latter engine was damaged beyond repair in an air raid in 1940, when she received a direct hit.

104

10
Northern Counties
of Ireland

In 1936 *The Railway Magazine* broke new ground. For many years previously the January number had been devoted to Scottish affairs, but not long after his appointment as Editor W. A. Willox was thinking of trying the experiment of a special Irish number. The threatened closing of some of the picturesque narrow gauge lines concurrently with a wave of enterprising traffic developments on the broad gauge had created an increased interest in Irish affairs. Above all, the appointment of Major Malcolm S. Speir as Manager of the Northern Counties Committee (NCC) section of the LMS, in 1931, had set in train a series of quite remarkable developments in the north. Willox suggested to me that a comprehensive article on the NCC would be acceptable for the first special Irish number, and knowing Major Speir personally he made the necessary introduction for me. It was something of a milestone in my own experience as an author, an assignment that took me in at the highest level.

The Major, as he was known everywhere on the NCC, was a tremendous enthusiast. On my first visit to Belfast he received me personally, not only so, but surrounded by a galaxy of chief officers, each of whom was briefed there and then as to the many features of interest I was to be shown. As always, my visits had to be made at weekends; but 'the 'Ulster Express' at 6.10pm from Euston, and the steamer from Heysham got me into Belfast by breakfast time on Saturday mornings, and each time, with whichever officer I had come to see, the Major would find time to dash in, wish me a good day, and then rush off on some urgent errand. His enthusiasm was doubly infectious, because he seemed to have transmitted it to every man on the line. My visits extended over many trips, and the article I wrote for the first 'Special Irish Number', May 1936, ran to two instalments. Furthermore there was no space to do more than make a passing reference to the locomotives, so that in readiness for a second Irish number a year later I wrote a detailed history of the locomotives, which Cecil J. Allen supplemented by including a number of my logs in his regular 'British Locomotive Practice and Performance' feature. The idea of a predominantly Irish issue did not please all readers, and I well remember the indignation of an aquaintance, a reverend gentleman who was himself something of a *Littérateur*, at the mere suggestion. I told Willox of this encounter, and in his pawky Aberdeenshire style of humour he replied: 'Oh well, we'll have an all-English number specially for him!'

When I first went to Belfast in the spring of 1935, the NCC was operating, very efficiently, with perhaps the most extraordinary variety of locomotives to be found anywhere in the British Isles. It had a history beginning with the appointment of Mr Bowman Malcolm as Locomotive Superintendent of the Belfast and Northern

Counties Railway in 1876. He himself was then no more than 22 years of age, but it was still more remarkable that he remained in the job for 46 years; even more so, when I first visited the NCC in 1935 *all* the engines that he introduced in that long innings were still in service, though a number had been substantially rebuilt. It was a fascinating job seeking out some of his older engines, at the far ends of byways in that northern county. The quest went on long after the genial summer weather had gone, and I well remember plunging round the little yard at Cookstown in deep snow to photograph the last of the so-called 'heavy compound' 4-4-0s in her compound condition. Bowman Malcolm's first engines, introduced in the year of his appointment, were conventional 2-4-0s, only three of them; but all were still in their original condition in 1935. I photographed the very first of them, No 23, in Coleraine shed. In 1890 however Malcolm began introducing 2-cylinder compounds on the Worsdell-von-Borries system, and until 1914 the line had none other than compounds, 2-4-0s, 4-4-0s and 0-6-0s.

Naturally my observations began with the expresses, and those running between Belfast and Portrush were the show trains of the line. The 'North Atlantic Express' was allowed 80min for the distance of 65.2miles, inclusive of one intermediate stop, and having regard to the intermediate gradients this required some smart running. The line between Ballymena and Portrush was single tracked throughout, but not only were all the passing stations equipped with the Manson apparatus for mechanical exchange of the tablets, but at each place the tracks were laid out for either direction running; one had been re-aligned to permit maximum speed through the loop, and the other was used in both directions by stopping trains. But although theoretically one could run through the loops at full speed there are always hazards with token exchanging. I remember one occasion in Scotland on the Stranraer line, when the engine gave a lurch at the psychological moment, and we clean missed the tablet. We had to stop, and the fireman ran back to collect it. On my very first footplate run from Belfast to Portrush, as we approached Ballymena, where single line working begins, the driver found the exchanging apparatus on the locomotive was jammed. Fierce blows with a hammer failed to free it in time, and again we had to stop, and collect the tablet by hand.

In 1935 the latest passenger engines on the NCC were the 2-6-0s of the 90 class. Since the war, and particularly after Bowman Malcolm's retirement in 1922 Midland, and then LMS influence had become strong on the NCC, and the 2-6-0s were a 5ft 3in gauge tender engine equivalent of the Fowler 2-6-4Ts of the 2300 class. I was already familiar with the sparkling performance of the latter, on the Euston-Watford suburban services. On Saturdays, the 8.53am non-stop from Watford to Euston originated at Tring instead of Northampton, and was a six-coach non-corridor set. The speeds made by the 2-6-4Ts, travelling bunker first, put completely in the shade the fast runs of the ex-LNWR express engines of Bletchley shed, attaining speeds up to 84mph on occasions. In conversation with some of the drivers I learned that the engines were linked up to very short cut-offs, inside 10%. When I came to ride the NCC 2-6-0s I found that some of them were worked in the same way. I went down on the footplate one evening with engine No 90 *Duke of Abercorn* on the 'North Atlantic Express', and the driver linked up to the altogether extraordinary position of 5% cut-off, with the regulator full open. As usual I sent in the draft of my report for vetting, and approval came in due course; but on my next visit to Belfast I learned from Willie Marshall, the very friendly Scots personal assistant to 'the Major', that the 5% cut-off had caused a storm of controversy in high quarters. Some said I was mistaken; others claimed it was impossible for an engine to work in such conditions, while a third faction thought that I had sufficient experience on locomotives not to be wrong. Eventually someone suggested that the best way to resolve all doubts was to ask the driver. He confirmed the 5% without hesitation, but added that engine No 90 was the only one of the class he would care to pull up so short.

The Moguls were not always used on the fast Portrush trains; in fact the very first run I had on the 'North Atlantic Express', on a Saturday, when it left Belfast at 12.50pm instead of 5.15pm, we were hauled by a 4-4-0 engine, one of the 6ft 'Castle' class of 1924, based on the Midland Class 2 superheated type, but adapted to the 5ft 3in gauge, and having 6ft diameter, instead of 7ft coupled wheels. They were excellent small power units, and a had a fine turn of speed. With the usual load of about 190 tons gross engine No 79 *Kenbaan Castle* made light of the job, and gave me the highest speed I ever logged on NCC metals, 76mph. Seven of these engines were built new by the North British Locomotive Company, but No 79 and two others of the class were built by the NCC in their own shops at Belfast. A number of the so-called 'heavy compounds' were also rebuilt at Belfast to conform with the 6ft 4-4-0s of 1924, and they did equally good work. After I had photographed the last of the 4-4-0 heavy compounds, No 63 *Queen Alexandra* at Cookstown in the winter of 1935, the next time I went to Belfast I was able to photograph the engine in her rebuilt form, still named *Queen Alexandra*, but with two cylinders 19in, diameter by 24in stroke, and conforming in every way to the 'Castle' class.

Very smart working was not confined to the Portrush trains. The boat expresses between Belfast and Larne Harbour were in every way top priority jobs, and with some the traffic arrangements were very tightly scheduled. The outward service in the morning connected with a train from Stranraer which conveyed through carriages for Euston, attached to the up 'Midday Scot' at Carlisle. The up 'North Atlantic Express' was advertised as running in connection with this service, with what might have been imagined as a rather hazardous 5min interval in Belfast, between arrival and departure. But actually there was no hazard because the 6-coach corridor dining car set of the 'North Atlantic Express' was also used for the boat train. The run of 24.3miles down to Larne Harbour was scheduled in 30min which, with the permanent speed restrictions on certain of the curves along the coast and at Larne Town intermediately required some very smart running, always made with 4-4-0 engines. These engines were usually of the largest, or 'Castle' class, but I have had runs with engines that were originally 'heavy compounds' but which were rebuilt with a smaller variety of superheated boiler.

On the final stretch of this short route, from Larne Town to the Harbour station the track of the former Ballymena and Larne narrow gauge line was alongside. I was too late to see passenger operation over this hilly and picturesque route, which in the short distance of 25 miles rises intermediately to a summit of 650ft above sea level, at Ballynashee, and then descends to little more than its initial altitude at Ballymena. It was closed to passenger traffic after the lengthy Irish railway strike of 1933. When I saw it in 1935 goods traffic was being worked by two rather ungainly 4-4-2T engines that had been built by Kitson's for the Ballycastle Railway in 1908. The really delightful period pieces among the narrow gauge stock of the NCC were the 2-4-2T compound engines designed by Bowman Malcolm in 1892 for the Ballymena and Larne Railway. These engines worked on the Worsdell-von Borries system, and the two cylinders, of different sizes were necessarily outside, with valves actuated by Walschaerts gear. In years prior to the 1933 strike a boat train service was operated from Ballymena in connection with the Stranraer steamers, and these little compound engines were required to run the 25 miles of very hilly road in the level hour. Two of them were supplied by Beyer Peacock & Co in 1892, when the line was the Ballymena and Larne section of the Belfast and Northern Counties Railway; two more of the same design were added by the NCC in 1908-9, and a final two, again to the identical design of 1892 in 1919-20. These four later engines were built at Belfast.

After the withdrawal of the passenger services on both the Ballymena and Larne, and on the Ballymena, Cushendall and Red Bay sections two of the compound tank engines were transferred to the Ballycastle Railway, and it was there that I saw them and travelled behind them. On arrival at Ballymoney, the main line junction for that delicious little narrow gauge line, most of the essential ingredients of the perfect Irish joke of a railway were apparent; passengers joined in lively badinage with enginemen and guard; the fireman would be solemnly re-coaling the engine from wicker baskets on the platform, and it seemed to the stranger that he had dropped in at some intimate family party. But apart from all the 'atmosphere' of the place the Ballycastle line was as efficiently run as any other part of the NCC. The run of $16\frac{1}{4}$ miles was booked to be run in 50min, including five intermediate stops, and in my experience the trains, composed of two large bogie coaches and whatever freight vehicles had to be conveyed, were run with clock-like punctuality. Like all NCC passenger engines, of whatever type or age, the compound 2-4-2T engines were painted in Midland red.

Major Speir, although a first class all-round manager was primarily an operating officer. He was trained on the Midland in the great days of Cecil W. Paget, but after further experience of railway operating in the USA he returned to his native Scotland in 1910 and entered the service of the Caledonian Railway. With an intermission on war service with the ROD, he remained in Scotland until his appointment to the NCC. From August 1924 he held the high office of Assistant General Superintendent of the Northern Division of the LMS. He was especially interested in signalling practice, and he added the safeguard on all main lines, of interlocking the starting signal for entry to each block section with the block instrument, so that the signal could not be cleared until 'lineclear' had been received on the block circuit. One of the most important installations of modern signalling in his time, for which I was personally responsible for design of some of the apparatus, was that put in at Coleraine in 1938. At that important junction, where the branch to Portrush diverges from the main line to Londonderry there were originally two signalboxes, one at each end of the station, and the decision to abandon one of them and concentrate all control from the north was accompanied by a decision to abandon single-line tablet work on the section to the first station to the south, at Macfin, where the Derry Central line comes in, and work it by track circuit control, and direction levers.

Just beyond Coleraine the main line to Londonderry crosses a multi-span viaduct over the River Bann, the seventh span of which from the Coleraine end was arranged for lifting on the bascule principle. The viaduct came within the track circuited area of Coleraine North signalbox, and interlocks were already in effect by which a tablet for the single line section between Coleraine and Castlerock could not be issued if the bridge were open. The converse interlocking also held good. This meant, that in the case of a down train tne bridge control was not released until the train had arrived at Castlerock, 5 miles away, and the tablet its engine was carrying inserted into the single-line block instrument there. With track circuiting in the Coleraine area, which included the Bann viaduct, the bridge control could be released as soon as the train had cleared the bridge itself, thus greatly lessening delay to river traffic. In 1935-7 there were five through trains a day between Belfast and Londonderry, each of a more intermediate character than the special Portrush expresses. The usually consisted of four or five coaches, including a buffet car, and a through carriage or carriages for Portrush, detached at Coleraine. For working light branch duties, such as these through carriages two of the oldest NCC locomotives were stationed at Coleraine, the Bowman Malcolm non-compound 2-4-0s of 1876.

It was a pleasant ride from Coleraine to Londonderry. At Castlerock the line is out on the coast, with a fine uninterrupted view of the north Atlantic; but then it cuts across a low promontory, like a northern equivalent of Dungeness, running out to Magilligan Point which is only a mile short of the Donegal shore opposite. Then at Limavady Junction the line is close to the shore again, now the broad inner reaches of Lough Foyle, and so it continues for the rest of the journey into Londonderry. There are some splendid prospects across the water to the Donegal hills on the opposite shore. So the line comes into its terminus by the water side. At the time of which I am writing the fastest train covered the $92\frac{3}{4}$miles from Belfast in 145min, calling at all stations between Coleraine and Limavady Junction, and then running fast into Londonderry. Two of the first non-compound 4-4-0s built by Bowman Malcolm in 1914 were stationed at Derry in the mid-1930s, both of them still in their original condition.

In all my travelling on the NCC however, and in visits to various engine sheds I had been intrigued by the comings and goings of the 2-cylinder compound tender engines, with their 'half speed' exhaust due to their having only two exhaust-beats per revolution. Enquiries in the locomotive department at Belfast revealed that Cookstown shed housed three locomotives, and that all of them were 2-cylinder compounds two 2-4-0s, and the one remaining 4-4-0. Moreover the 12.40pm through train to Belfast, and its balanced return working at 4.20pm was regularly worked by one of the 2-4-0s that had been rebuilt with one of the so-called 5-foot boilers; on the 2-4-0 chassis it made the engine look a massive little thing. I enquiried about a footplate pass. It was readily granted, but they suggested I did not go right through to Cookstown; I should, they thought, transfer at Magherafelt to the 5.35pm train for Coleraine, which went up the Derry Central line, and would be worked by another of the compound 2-4-0s. In high summer the trip was favoured by a day of the most beautiful weather and it was a thrilling experience to ride on what were tiny little engines compared to the large 4-6-0 and 4-6-2s then in general use in Great Britain.

In writing up the experiences afterwards I expressed the hope that one of these engines, as an example of the Worsdell-von Borries system of compound propulsion, might be preserved, because so far as I was aware the three 2-4-0s, Nos 51, 56 and 57, together with the 4-4-0 *Queen Alexandra* and the narrow gauge tank engines were the only remaining survivors. On the 4.20pm out of Belfast, on No 57 *Galgorm Castle*, for about half a mile from each of the starts I was treated to the rare spectacle of an engine being driven 'all out' — full regulator and full forward gear. It was rare, anyway, in the British Isles, and as we worked up to speed the noise of the exhaust, only two beats per revolution from the low pressure cylinder became tremendous. The action also, working up to a maximum speed of 64mph before our first stop at Dunadry, was hectic to say the least of it, 16 miles from Belfast in $22\frac{3}{4}$min with a 3-coach train of 85 tons all told. The running of the sister engine No 51 up the Derry Central line with only two coaches was also quite exciting in places, and today it is good to recall that I was able to include rides on these two veterans among the very many I have made on steam locomotives all over the world.

In making her opening run to Dunadry, the tough little *Galgorm Castle* had to climb the stiff gradients of the Greenisland loop line, in the ascent from waterside level by Belfast Lough to the summit at Kingsbog Junction, and for three miles the inclination is 1 in $76\frac{1}{2}$. Until 1933 the NCC was labouring under the disadvantage of a strange track alignment it had inherited from early days of the Belfast and Northern Counties Railway. To ease the gradients in climbing to the high ground at Ballyclare Junction the original line was taken, on nothing steeper than a short length of 1 in 97 to Greenisland. There trains for Portrush and Londonderry reversed direction, and continued on gradients of 1 in 101-107 to reach the summit. It was a cumbersome and time consuming operation, that also added three miles to the distance to be covered by a train bound for the north-west, The construction of the much needed direct line was carried out as one of several projects for relief of unemployment during the great depression of the early 1930s, with almost entirely unskilled labour — a masterpiece of technical planning and supervision in the field.

Above left: Northern Counties Committee (NCC) section, LMS; Class U2 4-4-0 No 87 *Queen Alexandra*, converted from one of Bowman Malcolm's 'heavy compound' 4-4-0s No 63, which bore the same name.

Left: One of the very efficient 2-6-0s of the NCC, here seen at Portrush, No 96 *Silver Jubilee*.

Top: 4-4-0 No 72 of Class U. This was one of a class of four, of which the first two, built in 1914, were the first non-compound main line engines built for the line for 24 years. The second two, of which No 72 was one, were added in 1922. They were notable in having Walschaerts valve-gear, inside. The engine in rear is No 83 *Carra Castle*.

Above: Narrow gauge train leaving Ballycastle. The engine is a 2-cylinder Worsdell-von Borries compound built for the Belfast and Northern Counties Railway, to Bowman Malcolm's design in 1909.

Above left: 2-cylinder compound 2-4-0 No 57 *Galgorm Castle* built in 1890, but since then fitted with a larger boiler. The name was originally carried by the first engine of the class, No 33.

Left: Another of the picturesque 2-cylinder compound 2-4-0s, here seen when the author was riding it, from Magherafelt down the Derry Central line to Coleraine in 1935.

Above: Another shot of No 51, and her 2-coach train, at Macfin, where the Derry Central joins the main line from Belfast to Londonderry.

Below: An example of Bowman Malcolm's first design, a non-compound 2-4-0 built in 1876, the year of his appointment as locomotive superintendent, when he was only 22 years of age.

11
Locomotives of Sir Nigel Gresley

By the time of the Railway Centenary celebrations, in 1925, Gresley was a confirmed and unshakeable exponent of 3-cylinder propulsion. In the paper he read on the subject, to the summer meeting of the Institution of Mechanical Engineers, in Newcastle, he quoted comparative test results from closely analogous 2 and 3-cylinder designs, both freight and passenger, which strongly supported his advocacy; and although the reputation of his express passenger Pacifics had suffered something of a jolt in the Interchange Trials with Great Western 'Castles' earlier in that same year, the unilateral manner in which the coal consumption figures had been revealed aroused no little sympathy for the LNER engines and their designer, who had undoubtedly come off second best in that interchange. It is frequently asserted that the great improvement made subsequently to the Pacific valve gear was a direct result of the disparity in performance revealed by the various comparative runs; but this was not so. Gresley was by no means satisfied with the performance of his Pacifics, and at the very time the interchange running was in progress the first experiments with a modified valve gear were beginning at Doncaster. How they were brought to a triumphant conclusion on engine No 2555 *Centenary* by the early months of 1927 I have told elsewhere; but so far as the present theme is concerned it meant that henceforth Gresley adopted 3-cylinder propulsion, with long lap, long travel valves for all his new designs, except the experimental water-tube boiler compound, with variations in the layout of the conjugated valve gear for the middle cylinder to suit the wheel arrangement of the particular engine.

So, there came the D49 class 4-4-0; the B17 4-6-0, or 'Sandringham' class; the V1 2-6-2T; the giant P2 2-8-2 'Cock o' the North' class, as well as development of the Pacific from the A1 through the A3 to the brilliant streamlined A4. Finally there came the V2, perhaps the most versatile and generally successful of them all, and the West Highland K4. Through the good offices of the late E. G. Marsden, who was then Information Agent of the LNER — a curious variation in title for a post normally known as Public Relations and Publicity Officer — I had more opportunities for riding on locomotives than on any other railway in the 1930s. Authority for granting engine passes rested with the three Running Superintendents, of the Southern, North Eastern, and Scottish Areas, and this once led to a mild internal fracas within the LNER. The scripts I wrote were all passed to Marsden for approval, and he in turn passed them, or so I believed, to the appropriate Area for their blessing. There was rarely any adverse comment or excisions. Willox was interested in my footplate journeying, and asked for a short account of one particular trip for *The Railway Gazette*; Marsden saw it, and approved, but some weeks later when it was in proof form Willox wrote to me and asked if Gresley had seen it. At that particular moment Marsden was away from the office, and I saw his assistant and showed him the proof. He, all unheeding, took the proof into the CME's office, and immediately I was told, all hell was let loose. Bulleid, who was then personal assistant to Gresley seized it, and stormed into the Assistant General Manager, the implacable Scot Robert Bell, saying 'Who gave this man permission to ride on our engines?' Bell, of course, did not know, but waited till Marsden returned, and then it was explained that authority had been given by the Running Superintendent, who was an independent senior officer himself responsible to the General Manager. It was nothing to do with Bulleid, or Gresley for that matter!

The East Coast trains were a fascinating study at that time. The accelerations of 1932 had put them in the very top flight of British train running; loads were constantly on the increase, and the sharing of the double-home turns between Kings Cross and Newcastle between the London and Tyneside sheds had bred a healthy competition between the Southern and the North Eastern Area men. For some time after the Grouping the North Eastern crews furnished with engines of Great Northern design for their principal express duties seemed to lose all sense of enterprise in their running. They would scrape along, barely keeping booked point-to-point times, and the slightest check was made the excuse for dropping behind time. One can appreciate that in a proud and individual concern like the old North Eastern Railway it had been galling to see their own engines passed over in favour of those from another, albeit an allied company. It was an attitude much the same as the repugnance shown on the former LNWR at the introduction of Midland compounds. But when it was arranged for the men of Gateshead and Heaton to learn the road to Kings Cross, and trains like the 'Flying Scotsman', and the 5.30pm Newcastle 'diner' were run by Cockneys and Geordies on alternate days things changed dramatically, and some of the finest runs I ever logged on the East Coast main line were made by Gateshead and Heaton men. It was an experience that was shared by all of us who were then travelling regularly over the route. The A1 and A3 Pacifics were used indiscriminately. The 'Flying Scotsman', and the 1.20pm from Kings Cross normally loaded to 15, though on both trains this included a triplet-articulated dining car set, weighing 84 tons. The tare load was between 480 and 485 tons, and as both trains were always well loaded the gross weight was around the 515 ton mark.

From the time of the 1932 accelerations the 1.20pm had the faster timing to Grantham, 114min for 107.5 miles. The following table summarises all my runs on heavily loaded down East Coast expresses from Kings Cross from 1932 until 1937 except for one, on which the Heaton engine on the down 'Flying Scotsman' was in trouble for steam, and stopped at Petersborough to take an Atlantic as pilot. I have quoted the net times to Grantham in each case.

Train ex-KX	Engine No	Name	Shed	Load tons gross	Net time min
5.30pm	2561	*Minoru*	Kings Cross	410	$106\frac{1}{2}$
5.30pm	2503	*Firdaussi*	Gateshead	425	$107\frac{1}{4}$
10am	2795	*Call Boy*	Haymarket*	480	$113\frac{1}{4}$
5.30pm	4472	*Flying Scotsman*	Kings Cross	505	111
1.20pm	2595	*Trigo*	Gateshead	515	$112\frac{1}{2}$
1.20pm	4476	*Royal Lancer*	Kings Cross	520	$114\frac{1}{2}$†
10.5am	2581	*Neil Gow*	Heaton	525	111

1.20pm	2744	*Grand Parade*	Kings Cross	530	$111\frac{1}{2}$
10am	2579	*Dick Turpin*	Heaton	550	$111\frac{1}{4}$
7.40pm	2557	*Blair Atholl*	Grantham	560	$118\frac{3}{4}$‡

*Non-stop to Edinburgh: Kings Cross driver
†Very severe westerly gale
‡The Aberdonian: schedule 124min

There were some great runs among the foregoing. The first was one of Driver Sparshatt's efforts. The 5.30pm was often delayed between Hatfield and Hitchin, and on the first run in the table very fast running was made afterwards to recover the loss. *Royal Lancer*, on the 1.20pm had to contend with a furious westerly gale and had a struggle to keep time, but what the North Eastern men could do was magnificently displayed by the two Heaton runs with engines Nos 2581 and 2579. The former was made during the period of the summer non-stop running of the 'Flying Scotsman' when the Heaton men had the 'Junior Scotsman', leaving at 10.05am. On the last run in the table the Grantham men on the 'Aberdonian' ran practically up to the winter schedule of the 'Flying Scotsman' as far as Peterborough, but then the engine was not extended, on the climb to Stoke. They passed the summit box, 100.1 miles from Kings Cross in $112\frac{1}{2}$min; but this was in high summer, and we were held up outside Grantham waiting for the equally heavy 'Highlandman' to clear.

These runs were typical of the kind of running that was being made throughout the line between London and Newcastle. It was noticeable particularly that there was little, if any falling off in performance towards the end of the long 268.3 mile through workings, and some of the finest runs I ever logged with the non-streamlined Gresley Pacifics were on the up road between Grantham and Kings Cross, with engines that had worked heavy trains through from Newcastle. Quite apart from the locomotive performance it was always a pleasure to travel in those crack East Coast trains. The massive teak-bodied coaches rode very smoothly, and gave a remarkable sense of well-being. On the 'Flying Scotsman' itself the first class dining car decorated in the style of a French restaurant of the Louis XIV period was a delight, never more so than on one occasion when I had been riding on the footplate on a very cold winter's day. I climbed down from the engine at Grantham, had a quick wash and tidy up, and then went through to the car to enjoy a hearty afternoon tea, while the weather outside turned into a blizzard! On the passenger services in the Southern Area, at any rate so far as the East Coast trains were concerned, the Gresley impact was confined to the Pacifics. The astonishing longevity of the ex-Great Northern Atlantics kept all others at bay, right up to the outbreak of World War II; but in the North Eastern there was a successful infiltration of an interesting Gresley design.

The D49 class of 3-cylinder 4-4-0 was the result of a need for locomotives of an intermediate power range that would take over duties performed by Atlantics and the larger 4-4-0s of pre-Grouping design. As things turned out very little capital was available on the LNER for provision of new motive power, and it was fortunate that the older engines had been maintained in very good order, and were in a position to carry on for many more years. So it befell, that although the new Gresley 3-cylinder 4-4-0s of the D49 class were introduced in both the North Eastern Area and Scottish Areas they were not superseding the existing Atlantics, though in certain cases they worked in the same links. The North Eastern had those fitted with the rotary-cam poppet valve gear, and replaced ex-NER 4-4-0s on the Leeds-Hull, and Leeds-Scarborough services. A prestige turn that they worked for some years was the morning Leeds-Glasgow express, as between Leeds and Newcastle. It was not normally a heavy train, carrying a regular load of eight coaches with a total weight of a little under 300 tons. It was booked non-stop over the 80.1 miles from York to Newcastle in 87min, and as such was a relatively easy job for a D49. Time was sometimes dropped on the initial allowance of 44min, to pass Darlington, 44.1 miles; but any such deficiency could easily be made up afterwards. I logged engine No 370 *The Rufford* on this job, with a gross load of 285 tons, and after taking $45\frac{1}{4}$min to pass Darlington she reached Newcastle $4\frac{1}{2}$min early ($82\frac{1}{2}$min from York) after a fast run down the Team Valley from Chester-le-Street.

In Scotland the D49s were those with the ordinary Walschaerts gear, and conjugated motion to operate the valves of the middle cylinder. They worked the lighter trains over the Waverley route to Carlisle, and on the East Coast main line from Edinburgh up to Aberdeen. But although they ran freely and quietly they never seemed to have quite the 'guts' of the North British Atlantics on the heavy gradients, but coupled to one of the GCR type 'Director' 4-4-0s they made a formidable combination on trains that loaded to 450 tons or more. They were frequently used on the weekend reliefs to the heavier trains, and did well with loads up to about 300 tons. I did however have one altogether outstanding run with one of them on the 1.20pm 'Scotsman' from Kings Cross, from Newcastle northwards, just before Easter. Although preceded by a relief train the 1.20pm was loaded to 16 from London. The expectation was that, as usual, this would be reduced to 10 at Newcastle, and the Haymarket Pacific normally rostered to take the train forward was put on to the relief, which was taking its full load through to Edinburgh. This left a D49, No 249 *Aberdeenshire* for the 10-coach main train, which as I told in Chapter 7 of this book, had some sharp timings. But when we arrived at Newcastle so many additional passengers were waiting to join the train that at a moment's notice it was decided to send the three leading coaches, which should have come off, forward to Edinburgh and our little D49 was faced with the task of hauling 13 coaches 412 tons tare, 435 tons full.

In addition to its regular stops at Alnmouth Junction and Berwick this train had conditional stops in Dunbar and Drem, and in such conditions it was inevitable that some time would be lost; but we were fortunate in having a driver, a spare link man at that time, who was outstanding in his skill as an engineman, and in his spirit of enterprise, none other than Norman McKillop, of Haymarket shed. He was then completely unknown, but in later years his exploits on the footplate, and his facility as a writer brought him fame. It is a pleasure to me to know I was the first to log one of his remarkable runs. With that big train he took us over the 34.8 miles to Alnmouth in $43\frac{1}{4}$min, and then on the succeeding 32.1 miles to Berwick, where the North Eastern Atlantics used to make such exciting running with the normal 340 ton train. *Aberdeenshire*, under McKillop's expert hand, made nearly as fast time with 435 tons. Onwards to Edinburgh, with both conditional stops to be made within an overall schedule of 67min for the remaining 57.5 miles it was inevitable that some time would be lost. With such a load it would have needed outstanding work from a Pacific to have run punctually in such conditions. The actual running time with the little D49 was 76min. It was nevertheless an exceptional performance from one of these engines, and they did not often have opportunities to shine so brightly.

It would be wrong to suggest that the express train services of the Great Eastern line were getting too much for the B12 superheater 4-6-0s of the 1500 class; because there was among the enginemen a tremendous sense of pride in the job, and a determination to remain on top of it, no matter how the engines had to be thrashed, and however much coal had to be shovelled. But it was the kind of working that could not be prolonged indefinitely. The difficulty lay in the limitation in axle loading, imposed over the line. Nevertheless the 3-cylinder system of propulsion and the improved balancing that it made possible, permitted the use of heavier engines, and the 'Sandringham' class of 4-6-0, with a nominal tractive effort of 25,380lb against the 21,969lb of the ex-GER 4-6-0s brought a welcome relief, particularly as some of the most severe duties, such as the outward bound 'Hook Continental' boat express, had been decelerated. An increase in time from 82 to 87min for the run of 68.9 miles from Liverpool Street to Parkeston Quay transformed an outstandingly hard duty — with loads of 450 tons — into a comfortably economic job. Some engines of the 'Sandringham' class were also stationed at Gorton, and worked down the Great Central line to Marylebone; but principal interest on that route began in 1936, when a new series of these 3-cylinder 4-6-0s was allocated to Leicester shed, and took up the workings so splendidly performed for many years by the ex-GCR Atlantics. The Leicester men took to them immediately, and were soon showing that the 'Sandringhams' could 'fly' as well as pull hard. They had never had opportunities for real speeding on the Great Eastern, but on the Great Central they were soon clocking up speeds of 90mph. They gained something of a reputation for rough riding, though personally in the course of various footplate journeys I never found them anything like so uncomfortable as the Thompson B1 4-6-0s that followed them after the death of Sir Nigel Gresley.

The policy of the LNER locomotive department in having engines that could handle the heaviest trains presented by the operating department stemmed naturally from the traditional Great Northern abhorrence of double heading; but while the A1 and A3 Pacifics had coped with increasing loads and increasing speeds south of Newcastle it was another matter on the Aberdeen route. The North British Atlantics continued to do a grand job, but the last straw, so far as the avoidance of double-heading was concerned was the introduction of third class sleeping cars on the principal night trains. In 1930 a few Pacifics were spared from Haymarket shed to work on the Aberdeen route. The maximum tonnages fixed for them were 480 tons northbound, but only 440 tons southbound. The latter was not enough to cope with the up 'Aberdonian' which was often considerably heavier. From their first introduction on this route Pacifics made a single return trip from Edinburgh to Aberdeen and back, being re-manned intermediately at Dundee in each direction. They went north on the 9.55am from Waverley, which, by the addition of the Glasgow portion at Kirkcaldy became a really heavy train. At Dundee however the load was reduced, and could have been taken unassisted by an Atlantic. Again, at Aberdeen it was no use keeping the Pacific back for the up 'Aberdonian', because its load was usually over the 440-ton limit. As the Pacific returned on the lightly loaded 5.35pm it was not a very satisfactory working. I logged No 2564 *Knight of Thistle* — phrased thus — and 2566 *Ladas* on these duties, but the running was undistinguished. The need on the Aberdeen road was for a locomotive that would take a tare load of 550 tons unassisted in the southbound direction, against 340 with an Atlantic and 440 with a Pacific and this is what Gresley produced in his magnificent P2 class 2-8-2s.

This is not a book about locomotive engineering, otherwise whole chapters could be written about the design, comparison between poppet and piston valves, tests in France, and the ultimate, premature, and tragic demise of these engines — an occurrence which one locomotive engineer, closely affected, stigmatised to me as 'pure bloody spite' — on the part of Gresley's successor. Here I am concerned only with the effect of the first two engines, Nos 2001 and 2002, on the running of the trains on the Aberdeen route in 1934-6, as I saw it personally. My first experience of *Cock o' the North* was actually between Kings Cross and Peterborough in July 1934 when dynamometer car trials were being run, from Doncaster, and although a heavy load of 585 tons were taken the engine did not need to be worked very hard to keep the schedule of the 4pm down from Kings Cross, then 87min for the 76.4 mile run. A month later I saw the engine at work in Scotland; it was then on the former Pacific turn at 9.55am from Waverley, but returning on the up 'Aberdonian'. When the two P2 engines went into regular service however they were double-manned and allocated to regular crews at Haymarket and Dundee. This meant an alteration to the workings so that *Cock o' the North* worked only between Edinburgh and Dundee, while *Earl Marischal* worked only north of Dundee, each engine making two return trips daily with the two regular crews on each alternating week by week on the early and late turns. These were:

Engine No 2001:	9.55am and 5.40pm	Edinburgh-Dundee
	2.38am and 9.30pm	Dundee-Edinburgh
Engine No 2002:	5.42am and 3.35pm	Dundee-Aberdeen
	10.20am and 7.35pm	Aberdeen-Dundee

The only train to be worked throughout by the P2 engines was the up 'Aberdonian', and in August 1935 I rode on the footplate from Aberdeen to Edinburgh when the load was 493 tons tare. Both engines made light of the job, but I was most impressed with *Earl Marischal*, which simply 'walked away' with that big train on the steeply inclined starts from Aberdeen, Stonehaven and Montrose. I had ridden earlier in the same day on the engine's first turn out from Dundee with her second crew, and they made equally light work of 480 ton trains in each direction. On the basis of that one day's experience I judged *Earl Marischal*, with piston valves, to be the better engine of the two, and I was not altogether surprised when *Cock o' the North* was converted, later, to have piston instead of poppet valves.

Amid all Gresley's introduction of spectacular new 3-cylinder engines in the 1930s, and in 1935, when I was enjoying the performance of the P2s in Scotland, the A4s and V2s had yet to come, the continuing phenomenon on the Great Northern section of the line was the running of the large boilered ex-GNR Atlantics. A present day reader might query the inclusion of a reference to these engines in a chapter titled 'Locomotives of Sir Nigel Gresley', when they were first introduced on to Great Northern metals before even Gresley had joined the staff at Doncaster; but it was entirely due to the modifications made to them, while he was still Locomotive Engineer of the GNR that transformed them into the astonishing engines we knew in the 1930s. It was the 32-element superheaters, in conjunction with a boiler pressure of 170lb sq in that was mainly responsible; and while the engines with 20in cylinders and piston valves were undoubtedly the best, those with slightly smaller cylinders, and slide valves were a remarkably good second best. The piston valve engines achieved virtual immortality in the working of the London-Leeds Pullman trains, and it is a pleasure to set down the overall results of my own journeys.

Leeds-Kings Cross 185.8 miles, Pullman trains

Engine No	Load tons full	Sch time min	Actual min sec	Net Time min	Net Average Speed mph	Max Speed mph
4436	285	193	193 00	188	59.4	85
4456	290	193	189 35	176	63.5	93
3280	295	205	209 55	$186\frac{1}{2}$	59.8	84
4444	300	195	195 25	190	58.8	82
3284	325	195	191 15	$181\frac{1}{4}$	61.5	88
4450	335	205	203 45	203	55.0	85
4444	335	205	194 45	190	58.8	$85\frac{1}{2}$

On the run with No 4456 I was on the footplate and saw how it was done, but on none of the other runs were the engine crews aware that a detailed record was being taken of their running.

There was another run, not included in the foregoing table, when on a winter's night of sleet and rain the pioneer large boilered Atlantic No 3251 was on the up 'Harrogate Sunday Pullman'. We were heavily delayed as far as Grantham, and passed through that station at 20mph. Then we got an undelayed run up to Kings Cross, and with a load of 325 tons the old warrior made a glorious run, covering the 105.5 miles from that very slow start in $104\frac{1}{4}$min. Schedule time from pass to stop was 111min, on which we gained nearly 7min. It was typical of the spirit embodied in the running of the Pullman trains at that time.

Left: Leeds-Glasgow express leaving York, on a very wet morning, hauled by 3-cylinder 4-4-0 No 211 *The York and Ainsty*. 'Hunt' class, with RC poppet valves.

Top: The piston valve version of Class D49, referred to as the 'Shires', engine No 264 *Stirlingshire* at Tweedmouth shed.

Above: Another of the 'Hunts', No 269 *The Cleveland* entering York with an express from the north.

Top left: Maximum loading from Kings Cross in 1935: the 4pm to Leeds, Bradford, and East Lincolnshire, 17 coaches, ready to leave behind Class A1 Pacific No 4477 *Gay Crusader*. The driver on that occasion was John Duddington of Doncaster shed who 3 years later made the world record speed of 126mph with *Mallard*.

Above left: One of the two Gresley P1 class 2-8-2 freight engines. No 2393, here seen climbing the 1 in 200 bank towards Stevenage with a maximum load coal train.

Left: At York, north end: the summer 'Junior Scotsman', 10.05am from Kings Cross, with engine No 2569 *Gladiateur*, waiting for the right away. On the southbound centre road is a Great Northern Atlantic No 4425.

Top: The up 'Flying Scotsman' leaving the Royal Border bridge, Berwick, hauled by Class A1 Pacific No 2571 *Sunstar*.

Above: One of Gresley's 2-cylinder 2-6-0s of Great Northern days, as adapted to work on the West Highland line, and named appropriately *Loch Eil*.

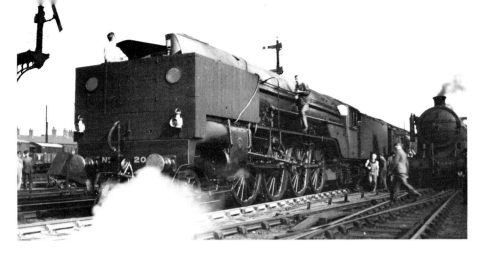

Top: The 2-8-2 No 2001 *Cock o' the North* at Peterborough, while undergoing dynamometer car trials between Kings Cross and Doncaster. Note the shelter round the front end to protect testing staff taking indicator diagrams and other data.

Above: The second 2-8-2 express engine No 2002 *Earl Marischal*, at Aberdeen, just before the author rode on the footplate southward to Dundee.

Left: The first of the celebrated V2 2-6-2s, No 4771 *Green Arrow*, on the 3.35pm Scotch goods. The train is waiting on the down slow line at Hitchin South for the down 'Coronation' streamliner to go ahead.

12
Scotland: Sou'West and the Caley

In 1930 Westinghouse won the contract for resignalling at St Enoch station, Glasgow. A good deal of on-site measurement would be needed in order that the fittings for some 100 sets of motor-worked points and many more colour light signals might be designed, and I was told that in due course it would be my job to go to Glasgow and get the necessary information. Several weeks passed, and then one Monday morning soon after I arrived at the London office I was advised that a site meeting was to be held in Glasgow on Wednesday, and that I should travel thence with certain senior officers of the company on Tuesday night. Although I was eager enough to go the date was just about as inconvenient as it could have been. It was high summer, and at the forthcoming weekend I had some extensive arrangements in connection with a garden fete at Woking. Still orders were orders, and in the brief time at my disposal I managed to delegate my responsibilities for the weekend, and hurriedly get together some effects. Unlike my other Westinghouse colleagues, who would be travelling up one night and back the next, my work on-site at St Enoch looked like taking at least a week, and probably more. Preparations were just one mad rush, and in the hurry, to my lasting regret, I forgot to pack my camera.

At that time St Enoch was a very interesting place from the locomotive point of view. There was an engine shed just outside the station where a great variety of the older Glasgow and South Western locomotives were based. Midland compounds had already taken over the principal Anglo-Scottish services via Kilmarnock and Dumfries, and these together with some of the Manson 4-6-0s were stationed at Corkerhill; but 4-4-0s of the main line and smaller-wheeled Clyde types were constantly on shed outside St Enoch, together with an occasional 4-6-4T of Robert Whitelegg's design. In the days that followed that first site meeting when I was constantly out on the line, how I kicked myself for not having a camera! I had a 'site office', complete with drawing board, in a wooden shed on the end of one of the platforms, and without playing truant from my lawful duties it would have been the easiest thing to nip across to the shed occasionally when an interesting locomotive literally posed itself ready for a photograph! Although there was to be a daylong site meeting with the local engineers on the forthcoming Sunday my own preliminary reconnaissance work had progressed far enough for me to make an evening trip to Ayr, and on the Saturday afternoon to go down to Greenock, and take a trip on one of the Clyde steamers.

The 5.10pm from St Enoch was something of a prestige train on the old G&SWR — why I could never quite understand. It was allowed 50min non-stop over the 41.4 miles to Ayr, over one of the easiest roads in the Kingdom. It was one of the duties for which Robert Whitelegg had introduced his huge and impressive looking 4-6-4Ts; but the loads were light and the performance less impressive than the look of the engines. It is true that there was a sharply curved, and junction-infested start out of St Enoch, with which I was rapidly becoming familiar, on foot! But once on to the joint line at Shields acceleration was painfully slow, and great respect was paid to the modest speed restriction at Paisley. The joint line, shared by Caledonian trains to Gourock and Wemyss Bay, was apt to get congested at times, even though it was quadruple tracked; and when the G&SW first put on the 50min trains to Ayr they routed them over the Canal Road to avoid checks from Caledonian locals on the joint road, even though their own line included much awkward curvature.

On the evening I went down to Ayr we had a Midland compound, No 913, for a train of 285 tons gross. At that time there was a heavy speed restriction near Kilwinning over the site of a colliery subsidence. It had been in operation for many months, but little attempt was made to get time in hand to offset its effect; and after we had taken nearly $12\frac{1}{2}$ minutes to cover the first 7.7 miles to Paisley acceleration on the very slight rising gradients to Lochside, nowhere steeper than 1 in 449, was so slow that in 7 miles we had not risen above 59mph. After we had passed the Kilwinning subsidence site, and passed Bogside we still had $12\frac{3}{4}$ minutes in which to cover the remaining 12.3 miles to Ayr, all on dead level track; but we failed to do it, creeping gradually up to the not very exciting sustained maximum of 60mph and reaching Ayr in 50min 55sec. I returned by a train that had the breathless schedule of 50 minutes for the 33.9 miles non-stop from Ayr to Paisley, on which a 250-ton train was hauled by an ex-G&SW 4-6-0 No 14656. Despite several slacks we managed to gain one minute, attaining a maximum speed of 53mph.

On my trip down to Greenock on the Saturday we had a Manson 0-6-0 goods engine that had been reboiled by Whitelegg and it was definitely not up to the job, but returning in the evening I was lucky enough to log one of the sparkling performances for which the small boilered Manson 4-4-0s were famous. From Princes Pier station the line climbs first at 1 in 70 and then at 1 in 98 for 5.7 gruelling miles, up the steep hillside giving a grand outlook over the Firth of Clyde; and up this, with a rousing tattoo from the exhaust the little engine lifted her 175-ton load with the utmost ease. At the top of the 1 in 70 speed had risen to 25mph and on nearing the summit of the bank just beyond Upper Port Glasgow signalbox we were doing 29mph. Then, although having coupled wheels no larger than 6ft 1in we dashed off down the bank through Kilmacolm to Bridge of Weir to reach a maximum of $73\frac{1}{2}$mph, and although slowing to 42mph to cross on to the main line from Ayr at Elderslie we completed the 17.8 miles from Princes Pier to Paisley in $28\frac{1}{4}$ minutes, nearly 3 minutes inside schedule time.

On the London expresses from St Enoch, still traditionally known as the 'Pullmans', on the Sou'West line, loading regulations seemed very strict for the Barrhill bank, with its $3\frac{1}{4}$ miles of 1 in 67-70, and all the time I was working at St Enoch I did not once see one of those trains leave without a pilot, although the tare loads were always well below 300 tons. There were plenty of ex-G&SW 4-4-0s on hand, but within my observations ex-Caledonian 4-4-0s of the Pickersgill type were always used for those main line piloting duties. At the end of my stint I went south by the 12 noon train, and the Midland compound and its pilot, with a gross trailing load of 295 tons fell from 46 to $27\frac{1}{2}$mph in the ascent of the Barrhead bank. South from Kilmarnock, the compound on its own took exactly the 72min scheduled for the 58 miles to Dumfries, and leaving there a minute late made this up by running the remaining 33.1 miles to Carlisle in 41min, and completing the journey from Glasgow in precisely the 2hr 37min scheduled. It was not a very exciting trip, and when I saw that the train was to be double-headed southward from Carlisle I got out, and waited for the 'Midday Scot'.

Two months later, when I went north to join my parents, who were on holiday at Stonehaven I took the 10.18am north from Leeds and had one of the most exhilarating runs that had yet come my way. The work over the Midland line was good enough, with an ex-LNWR 'Claughton' 4-6-0 making a very vigorous run throughout from Leeds to Carlisle; but it was on the Sou'West line, when compound No 913 took over — the same engine that had given me the dull and lethargic trip on the 5.10pm from St Enoch to Ayr — that the work at times bordered on the phenomenal. For this 4-4-0 engine had to take forward a gross trailing load of 375 tons, and no pilot was taken at any point, even for the steeply graded final stage from Kilmarnock into Glasgow. I have many times previously described, eulogised, and analysed scientifically this magnificent performance; but in retrospect it was characteristic of the steam era, in which so much depended upon the personality of the driver and fireman. How otherwise could one explain the difference in the running of the same engine, between the poverty stricken drifting along on the 5.10pm to Ayr, and this lion-hearted classic on the 1pm from Carlisle to St Enoch. For the record, I set out the bare details of this superb run; but to have experienced it personally and listened to it, from the carriage, was the thrill of a lifetime. On the two sections where checks occurred the net times were $67\frac{1}{2}$ and 35 minutes. To pass New Cummock on time after the long, grinding ascent from Dumfries was an outstanding effort, and although time was lost on the very stiff ascent out of Kilmarnock we should have made up the $1\frac{1}{2}$ minutes arrears at Barrhead but for the final checks.

1pm Carlisle — St Enoch 30 August 1930
Load: 350 tons tare, 375 tons full
Engine: 3-cylinder compound 4-4-0 No 913

Dist Miles		Sch min	Actual min sec
0.0	Carlisle	0	0 00
8.6	Gretna Junction	11	11 40
17.5	Annan	21	21 30
15.6	Dumfries	20	19 00
14.2	Thornhill	17	18 50
26.1	Sanquhar	32	33 10
36.9	New Cumnock	45	45 10
48.6	Mauchline	57	56 55
—	—	—	sig & pw checks
58.0	Kilmarnock	69	70 30
10.0	Lugton	16	17 50
16.8	Barrhead	24	25 25
—	—	—	pw checks
22.5	Strathbungo	31	33 35
—	—	—	sig stop
24.4	Glasgow St Enoch	35	39 25

Although there had been a considerable infusion of new standard LMS types to the Caledonian line by 1930, north of Glasgow and Edinburgh it was only on through trains from the south that the Midland compounds had taken over, on double-home turns from Kingmoor shed, Carlisle. Southbound the trains they worked were the 6.45pm to Euston, the 3.30pm up Postal and the up 'Royal Highlander', leaving at 7.50pm. The first two were quite light trains from Aberdeen, but the 'sleeper' usually needed a pilot, often one of the last remaining 4-4-0s of the first 'Dunalastair' class, No 14316. On the LMS side the principal interest north of Perth was in the working of the ex-Caledonian engines, and apart from taking many photographs I made a number of short trips. The steep gradients between Aberdeen and Forfar provided excellent opportunities for assessing the capacity of the various types, often with quite substantial loads. The Pickersgill 4-4-0s, and the McIntosh superheater variety of the 'Dunalastair IV' class were used turn and turn about, and I found the McIntosh engines consistently the better in hard hill climbing, and much faster runners downhill.

Between Glasgow and Perth the handsome Pickersgill outside cylinder 4-6-0 were used; but they were the most awful sluggards. I have dreary recollections of them laboriously making their way up to 50 or 55mph on level track, and they rarely touched as much as 60mph downhill. Occasionally one of them would come up to Aberdeen on the mid-afternoon train, with a light load of only 5 or 6 coaches. The return working was on the 5.35pm which in later LMS days was named 'The Granite City'. But there was an astonishing difference one week when that afternoon train from Perth was worked by one of the two pioneer McIntosh large boilered 4-6-0s, No 49, or 14750 as she was in 1930. Those two most beautiful engines were the predecessors of the 'Cardean' class, and they were real 'flyers'. When I discovered No 14750 was to be on the 5.35pm up I went into Aberdeen to travel behind her back to Stonehaven, and I was not disappointed. She sailed up on to the cliffs by Cove Bay with hardly a sound from the exhaust, and then flew down through Muchalls touching 70mph. I was sorry not to be able to go further south behind her that day; but high tea was waiting in Stonehaven, and in those family days punctuality at meals was a must! The astonishing difference between those McIntosh 4-6-0s of 1903, and the Pickersgill's of 1916 have always puzzled me. Of course the later engines like the 4-4-0s were most massively built, and were very low on repair costs; but the valve setting cramped their style to a most unbelievable extent.

In later years I had some further illuminating experience of Caledonian locomotive working on the Callander and Oban line. There again Pickersgill had designed a special 4-6-0 for the job. In 1902 McIntosh had built a class of 4-6-0s with very small wheels specially for climbing the heavy gradients and they were very successful. The line is unusual compared to the far-famed West Highland, and equally to the Highland itself. For although the Callander and Oban had some very steep gradients, including stretches of 1 in 50 long enough to rule the load, there were also some considerable lengths of virtually level track in between, on which the schedules required some brisk running, There was, for example, a stretch of 7 miles beside Loch Lubnaig, from St Bride's crossing through Strathyre, and after the fearsome 'gable' to the 941ft summit at Glenoglehead had been negotiated there was another 8 miles from Luib to beyond Crianlarich. With the relatively light loads of the early 1900s the small wheeled McIntosh 4-6-0s skipped along happily enough; but when heavier loads, corridor coaches, and the occasional Pullman car demanded more powerful locomotives Pickersgill came up with another veritable enigma.

His 'Oban' 4-6-0, introduced in the last years of the Caledonian Railway, was an extraordinarily feeble thing. The cylinders were outside, fed by a very small non-superheated boiler, and the valve gear was Walschaerts. Now if there is a class of duty in which a well-designed Stephenson link motion excels it is in slogging up heavy gradients. The drawing office that served McIntosh so well made no mistake about the first Oban 4-6-0s, but the poor little Pickersgills were not so well served. I made some footplate runs with them in 1937, and found them quite feeble. They rode very comfortably and smoothly, but that boiler and firebox simply could not produce the steam. It was not that they were bad steamers; the boiler simply could not produce enough to do the job. It was very noticeable how quickly the pressure rose once the regulator was closed, either for a station stop, or a spell of downhill coasting.

By that time sufficient Stanier 'Black Five' 4-6-0s had been allocated to the Highland main line to make the 'Clan' class 4-6-0s redundant, and all eight of them were transferred to Oban shed. They took over all the principal passenger workings on the line, and ran through from Oban to Glasgow (Buchanan Street) on a double-home basis. During the summer tourist season the loads of many of the trains were heavy, especially the day excursions run from Glasgow on Sundays; and although the Pickersgill 4-6-0s were sometimes used for piloting, the most favoured engines for that kind of duty was the ex-Caledonian Drummond 0-6-0 — tough, and splendid working little engines. The combination of those engines with the 'Clans' could easily have been mistaken for an all-Highland partnership, because those Caledonian 0-6-0s, by Dugald Drummond, were the prototypes of Peter Drummond's 'Barneys' in the Highland. When both were painted in the unlined black of the LMS, and they both had plain dome covers, instead of the Drummond type with safety valves on the top it was indeed hard to tell the two classes apart.

The 'Clans' did a splendid job of work on the Oban line. There was little comfort, or refinement in their cabs, and the Balornock men who worked them on certain turns compared them very unfavourably to the Stanier 'Black Fives', and 'Jubilees'; which was natural enough. But the main point about the 'Clans' was that they would *steam*: steam reliably and constantly against the most severe and continuous thrashing. I came up from Oban one evening on the 5.15pm train, and with a gross load of 375 tons even a 'Clan' needed piloting. We were given a Pickersgill, and out of curiosity I rode her as far as Crianlarich. One thought of rice puddings and their skins! That poor old pilot was taking a very meagre share of the load, and on each of the banks down came the boiler pressure. At one time we had got no more than 110lb sq in on the clock and our fireman drew my attention to the 'Clan' behind us, roaring its heart out as only those engines could when in full cry. She was taking at least two-thirds of the load, and despite the thrashing she was taking the 'white feather' was showing constantly from her safety valves.

I changed over to *Clan Mackinnon* at Crianlarich, and was thrilled at the way she went up the 1 in 69 from Luib to Killin Junction, and thence up to the summit at Glenoglehead. There we crossed the corresponding train from Glasgow, and the enginemen changed over. It was then that I heard some Balornock opinions of the 'Clans'. The pilot came off at Balquhidder, and *Clan Mackinnon* had to take the full load as far as Stirling, where it would be reduced somewhat by the detaching of the Edinburgh portion. It was, of course, on the faster stretches of the main line that the 'Clans' showed up less favourably, particularly since the Stanier engines had come upon the scene. But even on the main line between Stirling and

Glasgow a 'Clan' could leave some of the big Pickersgill 4-6-0s standing. Not for nothing did the latter unfortunate engines gain the nickname of the 'Greybacks'!

On the mountain sections of the Callander and Oban line I recorded some remarkable hill-climbing performances with the 'Clans'. It was symptomatic of the affection in which they were held that the local men at Oban nearly always referred to them by their names, rather than numbers — omitting the word 'Clan'. Down at the shed one hard them referred to as *Fraser, Stewart, Mackenzie*, just as if they were fellow railwaymen. At different times I rode *Clan Munro, Clan Mackinnon* and *Clan Mackenzie*, and the general concensus of opinion was that *Mackinnon* was the best of them all. It was a very strong engine on the banks, though the heaviest task I saw set to one of them was to *Clan Chattan*, when a load of no less than 302 tons tare had to be taken westward from Balquidder without a pilot. There is a gradient of 1 in 60 right off the platform end, and it continues for 5 miles without the slightest easing. Without any slipping, but with a tremendous blast from the exhaust *Clan Chattan* gradually accelerated this load to 16mph. I would like to have seen how she continued through to Oban, but I was bound for Killin that day, and alighted from the train at Killin Junction.

During a holiday in those regions in 1937, I noted several other interesting engines. One of them was another splendid Highlandman, the *Urquhart Castle*, though I did not get an opportunity of travelling behind her, while at Balquhidder one day I came across, on a goods train, what at first I thought to be one of the smaller-wheeled goods 4-6-0s of the McIntosh era on the Caledonian, characterised by the usual large boiler and very shapely mountings; but on checking the number I realised it was one of the original McIntosh 'Oban' 4-6-0s that had been rebuilt with one of the large boilers. I wondered to what extent rebuilding had been a success, because in not a few cases of similar treatment the balance of the design had been upset, as I mentioned earlier in this book, when referring to the rebuilding of some of the Highland 'Loch' class 4-4-0s. I never saw that rebuilt 'Oban' 4-6-0 again, and cannot recall any details of her performance being published.

The last time I went to the Oban line before the outbreak of World War II was early in 1939, and then the Stanier 'Black Five' 4-6-0s were in full possession. It was early in the year, and the loads were not heavy, and those fine engines, brand new, simply romped up the banks. In due course *Clan Mackinnon* found her way back to the Highland main line and was at Inverness until after nationalisation. She was the last of the class to remain in service, long enough to receive a BR number.

Below left: The second of the Pickersgill 4-6-0s Caledonian type built by the LMS in 1925, and painted red. This photograph was taken at Kingmoor sheds when the engine was in plain black.

Top: Two Scottish Moguls at Carlisle: in front one of Peter Drummond's ex-G&SW type; No 17829 illustrated was the last but one of 11 engines built in 1915 by the North British Locomotive Company. In rear is a McIntosh 2-6-0 of the Caledonian, built 1912, and the first Mogul to run in Scotland.

Above: One of the ill-starred Pickersgill 3-cylinder 4-6-0s of 1921, No 14801, at Kingmoor, in 1933. This engine was originally Caledonian No 957.

Below: Two McIntosh 4-4-0s at Edinburgh Princes Street in 1932; on the left a 'Dunalastair III' and on the right a superheated 'Dunalastair IV'. Although both engines were painted black neither carried smokebox number plates.

Above: A train from Crieff climbing the bank from Lochearnhead to Balquhidder, hauled by a McIntosh 0-6-0 No 17604. The track of the Oban line, climbing to Glenoglehead is on the hillside behind the trees.

Below: An interesting rebuilt Caledonian 4-6-0 at Balquhidder in 1937: one of the McIntosh 'Oban' type 4-6-0s, No 14606, rebuilt with large boiler.

Bottom: 'Clans' on the Oban line: Glasgow to Oban express entering Strathyre station hauled by No 14768 *Clan Mackenzie.*

Right: Glasgow-Oban express at Balquhidder in 1938 hauled by a small Caledonian 0-6-0 No 17397, and an ex-Highland 'Clan' class 4-6-0 No 14767 *Clan Mackinnon.*

Below right: Locomotives of the 5.15pm up from Oban just before starting: a Pickersgill 'Oban' type 4-6-0, on which the author rode, and Highland 4-6-0 No 14767 *Clan Mackinnon.*

Bottom right: The return Sunday day excursion from Glasgow to Oban beginning the heavy climb out of Dalmally, hauled by a Drummond 0-6-0, and a 'Clan'. The quintuple-peaked mountain in the left background is Ben Cruachan.

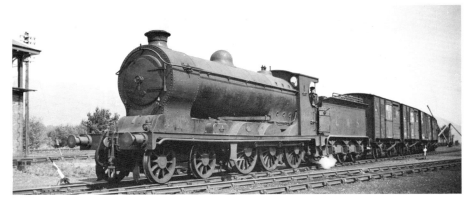

Top: The famous Caledonian 4-2-2 No 123 in 1932 in her last days as an ordinary traffic department engine. She was stationed at Perth, painted black and numbered 14010, and worked local trains between Perth and Dundee.

Below: LNER, Great North of Scotland section: a stopping train for Ballater leaving Aberdeen in 1929, hauled by one of the James Johnson 4-4-0s of 1893-8 vintage, No 6906.

Above: One of the final batch of McIntosh mixed traffic 4-6-0s of the Caledonian, distinguished by having side-windowed cabs: No 17913, photographed at Perth in 1932.

13
GWR: Days with 'Castles' and 'Kings'

For some years after my spell at Chippenham in 1926 my travelling, both for businesss and holiday purposes lay outside Great Western territory. I had not much time to spare for purely railway observation and most of it was spent in the north, and in travelling thence. While my parents still lived at Barrow-in-Furness however there were still those long bank-holiday weekends, and from 1928 I used the Great Western route to Shrewsbury, or to Chester, on several occasions on the first stage of my journey north. It involved a somewhat grisly series of semi-fast connections to get from Crewe to Carnforth in the early hours of the morning, but it gave me an opportunity to travel on one of the most important of the two-hour Birmingham expresses, the one leaving Paddington at 6.10pm. From 1928 also, that train was usually hauled by one of the then-new 'Kings'. The eve of a bank-holiday added to the spice of the occasion, with loads heavier than usual, and as there were ample timetable margins ahead of that train it was seldom troubled by the signal checks that so often beset other important services at holiday times. My first run was however a big disappointment, as the latest engine of the class, No 6019 *King Henry V*, then brand new, lost time. Perhaps it was a little too new to be thrown 'into the breach'.

Runs with 'Castles' had given me nothing very special up to that time, either. All of these had been in the up direction, on either the 4pm or the 6pm from Birmingham. The latter had a curious working. One engine worked south from Shrewsbury to Leamington, and then continued with that portion of the train that went via Oxford. An Old Oak engine then coupled on to the Bicester route portion, which called only at High Wycombe. Normally this was a fairly easy job for a 'Castle'. Four runs gave the following results on the Leamington-High Wycombe stage, booked in 64min start to stop for 60.8 miles.

Engine No	Name	Load tons full	Time min sec	Max Speed mph
4098	*Kidwelly Castle*	280	60 00	82
5010	*Restormel Castle*	270	60 00	$82\frac{1}{2}$
5010	*Restormel Castle*	350	68 05*	84
4092	*Dunraven Castle*	375	63 50	$77\frac{1}{2}$

*$63\frac{1}{2}$min net

On another occasion when I travelled on the 4pm up from Birmingham, loaded to 420 tons from Leamington we had engine No 4016 *Knight of the Golden Fleece*, rebuilt as a 'Castle' but suffered a series of delays and eventually took $110\frac{1}{4}$min instead of the 91 scheduled from Leamington to Paddington.

Turning now to the 'Kings', on that first journey of mine on 3 August 1928 we had a gross load of 480 tons out of Paddington, reduced by the detaching of one slip coach at Bicester and two at Banbury to gross loads of 450 and 385 tons on the successive stages. A signal check at West London Junction cost us about $1\frac{1}{2}$min, but the lateness increased to 5min, at High Wycombe, 7min at Princes Risborough, and then we continued at 7 to $7\frac{1}{2}$min behind time to Banbury. From Fenny Compton onwards we made a dash for Leamington reaching $86\frac{1}{2}$mph down the Fosse Road bank, but we were still $6\frac{1}{4}$min late in. The driver held his own onwards to Wolverhampton, with the reduced load of 385 tons, but it was not an impressive performance. Some allowance must undoubtedly be made for the driver and fireman being unfamiliar with the greatly enlarged type of locomotive.

At Whitsun 1929 I tried the same train again and it was a very different story, with the same engine. This time no slip portions were carried and the heavy load of 475 tons was taken through to Wolverhampton. Once again we were checked, in fact brought to a dead stand before clearing the Old Oak Junctions, and the loss of time was fully 4min; but after that the going was splendid, and the 78.6 miles from Greenford to Milepost 105 were covered in exactly 77min. Leamington was reached in 94min — 3min late it is true — but only 90min net. With that big load it was not possible to keep the sharp 26min allowance for the 23.3 miles on to Birmingham, and $1\frac{3}{4}$min were lost; but on the final stage $1\frac{1}{4}$min were gained on the 20min timing for the 12.6 miles to Wolverhampton. The train was there reduced to a modest 285 tons, and was taken forward by *two* Moguls, Nos 6376 and 4342, instead of the usual 'Saint' or 'Star'.

Heartened by the excellent results of this somewhat unorthodox route from London to Barrow I tried it again a year later, and was rewarded by one of the finest runs I ever noted on the Great Western Railway. I was living at Ealing at the time, and on my digs-ward journeys each evening from Kings Cross, via the Metropolitan line and Bishops Road, I had noted that No 4088 *Dartmouth Castle* was on the 6.10pm night after night. So she was, also, on the Friday before Whitsun, but like *King Henry V* a year earlier she had to take a load of 475 tons, unrelieved by any slip portions, right through to Wolverhampton. As before, there were signal checks before Old Oak; but they were not serious, and thereafter we had a clear road right through to Tyseley. Believe it or not, we were $1\frac{1}{4}$min *early* on arrival at Leamington, after a sustained performance of outstanding merit. It is true that some of the speed restrictions were interpreted rather liberally, such as 50mph through High Wycombe instead of 35, $64\frac{1}{2}$mph at Ashendon Junction, instead of 50, and 59mph at Aynho Junction, instead of 55; but the train rode smoothly enough at these points, and between times we ran very hard, both uphill and down. The maximum speed was $83\frac{1}{2}$mph at Haddenham.

With such a load it was not surprising that we lost a little time between Leamington and Birmingham, but of the $5\frac{1}{2}$min of lateness with which we arrived at Snow Hill, $3\frac{1}{4}$min of it was due to excess station time at Leamington. We ran splendidly on to Wolverhampton, regaining $1\frac{3}{4}$min of lost time, and the final check up for the driver showed 2min gain, 3min loss, and $1\frac{3}{4}$min gain on the three stages — a magnificent piece of running. My next run on that train, in normal loading conditions, was tame by comparison. Engine No 6017 *King Edward IV* had a load of 430, 400 and 330 tons on the three stages, and with only one slight check dropped $\frac{1}{2}$min to Leamington, $91\frac{1}{2}$min for the 87.3 miles from Paddington; but with only 330 tons it was possible to make a fast run onwards to Birmingham in $25\frac{1}{4}$min and to arrive in Snow Hill in 119min 55sec overall from Paddington.

I used the 9.10am down from Paddington on one or two occasions. This was also a two-hour train, making one stop at High Wycombe, and running the 84.1 miles thence to Birmingham in 88min. This train was worked by Old Oak engines and men, and the running was not as enterprising as one might have expected. One of my best runs was with No 4099 *Kilgerran Castle*, with a load of 360 tons from the start, 322 tons from Banbury, and 285 from Leamington. We left High Wycombe on time, but lost a minute to Ashendon Junction. The conditional stop at Bicester was made, and with a moderate permanent way check to follow we were $7\frac{3}{4}$min late past Banbury. But with the much lighter load, especially that from Leamington, the subsequent running did not compare with that of *Dartmouth Castle*, and we were still 5min late on arrival in Birmingham. I could not help feeling we could have been very nearly punctual if the driver had been so minded.

About the same time I noted also some very lack-lustre running by 'Castles' on the South Wales service. On the 8.55am down from Paddington, No 4097 *Kenilworth Castle* with a 385-ton train, leaving Reading 2min late lost another $4\frac{1}{2}$min to Stoke Gifford East Box — 75.5 miles in $82\frac{1}{2}$min — and with no more than one more moderate permanent way check took a total of $112\frac{3}{4}$min for the 97.4 miles from Reading to Newport. Net time was just about the 105min scheduled, but the work lacked anything in the way of sparkle. Returning the same evening on the 6.37pm from Cardiff, with *Lulworth Castle* and a 300-ton load, with no more than two slight checks we took $77\frac{1}{2}$min from Newport to Swindon, 56.1 miles, instead of 68min scheduled; and after this rather miserable show, with a reduced load of 270 tons made up no time on the very easy timings thence to Paddington.

Mention of *Lulworth Castle* however brings me to my first trip on the 'Cheltenham Flyer' after it had been accelerated to a 70min run from Swindon to Paddington. Between October 1929 and December 1934 I made eight runs on the train. To advertise this fastest of all their runs the GWR issued excursion tickets at 5/- (25p) return from Paddington, outward by the 1.18pm and back with the 'Flyer'. I was constantly surprised at how few railway enthusiasts availed themselves of this tempting offer. All my own runs were made on Saturday afternoons, the first three in the accompanying table when the schedule was 70min and the remainder after its acceleration to 65min. They are tabulated in chronological order rather than of ascending load, and the first was in some ways the most brilliant of all. After a relatively easy start we ran at a continuous $83\frac{1}{2}$ to $86\frac{1}{2}$mph throughout from Steventon to Tilehurst. The driver eased considerably after Reading. No 3 was poor, on a winter's night, and No 5, on a summer day was made amid the rush of much other traffic. The others were all excellent, especially the last, on a rough December night, amid rain and sleet.

'The Cheltenham Flyer'

Run No	Engine No	Name	Load tons full	Actual Time min sec	Net Time min	Max Speed mph
1	5003	*Lulworth Castle*	275	67 15	66	$86\frac{1}{2}$
2	4090	*Dorchester Castle*	220	69 15	$69\frac{1}{4}$	78
3	5001	*Llandovery Castle*	230	76 15	73	75

4	5018	*St Mawes Castle*	230	64 35	$61\frac{1}{2}$	85
5	4082	*Windsor Castle*	270	68 10	64	82
6	111	*Viscount Churchill*	230	63 55	64	$85\frac{1}{2}$
7	5015	*Kingswear Castle*	235	62 55	63	$83\frac{1}{2}$
8	5025	*Chirk Castle*	270	62 15	$62\frac{1}{4}$	$86\frac{1}{2}$

In 1935, as Easter approached, I felt the need to get away from railways for a while. In my professional work I had been much involved in design of apparatus for two of the largest signalling contracts Westinghouse had received for some years, and at weekends I had been equally involved with footplate work on the northern lines. I decided to renew acquaintance with some of my old haunts in west Cornwall. The spring flowers would be at their best, and if the weather remained good the glorious cliff walks in the Lands End district would be exhilarating. True, I should travel down to Penzance on the 'Cornish Riviera Express', but for once I contemplated this journey as a means for getting to the other end, rather than a potential source of interesting data. With a plethora of relief trains, excursions and such on the line one could hardly expect, or so I thought, a very punctual run. I had an old favourite among my topographical books, *Highways and Byways in Devon and Cornwall* with me; I bought newspapers and a copy of *Country Life* at Paddington, and beyond noting that the train was divided, and that we had, for 'The Limited', the relatively light load of 440 tons I settled down into a facing window corner to relax and enjoy the ride.

Alas for such intentions of detachment! We went out of Paddington like the proverbial bomb; by West Drayton my stop watch was out clocking speeds rising in to the mid- 70s and I found myself logging in detail what proved to be a most exhilarating run. It was the first time I had travelled to the west since the construction of the Westbury and Frome by-pass lines, and I was impressed with the beautiful evenness of the speed. Of course, with a load of no more than 440 tons the engine was not unduly pressed, even though there were no slip portions on this first division of the train, and the full load had to be taken through to Exeter; but the average speeds from the start to various points en route are indicative of our progress: 60.8mph to Reading; 61.8 to Savernake; 63.8 to Heywood Road Junction; 61.8 to Castle Cary, and 62.7 to Taunton . At the latter, 142.7 miles from Paddington in $136\frac{1}{2}$min we were comfortably ahead of time, with $33\frac{1}{4}$min left to complete the remaining 30.8 miles to Exeter. Speed was indeed allowed to fall to 29mph at Whiteball summit, and we ran for much of the ensuing descent without steam. Exeter was reached $1\frac{1}{4}$min early in $168\frac{3}{4}$min from Paddington.

One coach was detached at Exeter leaving a train of 376 tons tare, 405 tons full to go on to Plymouth. The maximum unpiloted load for a 'King' over the South Devon line was 360 tons, and although it was evident that this particular engine, No 6016 *King Edward V*, was in top form I fully expected a stop to be made at Newton Abbot for a bank engine. It was time to relax again, or try to. I went into the corridor and enjoyed the leisurely run through Starcross, and along the ever-fascinating Dawlish-Teignmouth stretch; but as we approached Newton Abbot there was evidently no intention of stopping. We ran through at 33mph and once clear of the junctions at the west end the exhaust suddenly opened up in a roar. Acceleration was rapid, in a positive charge at the formidable Dainton Bank. That load of 405 tons is the heaviest I have every heard of taken unpiloted by a steam locomotive over the Dainton and Rattery inclines. The minimum speeds were $21\frac{1}{2}$

and $23\frac{1}{4}$ mph respectively, and a commendable feature of this part of the run was that the driver made no attempt to gain time downhill. Speed did not exceed 56mph on the descent from Dainton Tunnel to Totnes. But with such powerful work up the banks time was well in hand. The advertised time for the 52 miles from Exeter to Plymouth was 72min and despite a signal check at the finish — the first, and only one of the whole journey from Paddington to Penzance — we completed this part of the run in $69\frac{1}{2}$min.

We then exchanged *King Edward V* for *Llantillo Castle*, and continued into Cornwall with an unchanged load. Since I made my first journeys on 'The Limited' its burden had been increased by a through carriage for Newquay. This could, of course, have been detached at Truro, and sent round via Perranporth; but the insertion of a stop at Par not only permitted an arrival nearly one hour earlier at Newquay, but also, for those who were prepared to make the short intervening distance by road, an excellent afternoon connection to Fowey. With these heavy trains I found the working of the 'Castles' in Cornwall very interesting. For what was essentially a high speed engine the succession of stiff banks with no chance of developing the kind of sustained speed in which they excelled I could not help feeling that they were far from ideal engines for the job. *Llantilio Castle* lost a little time to Par, and then with her load reduced by one coach, regained it on the allowance of 33min for the 19.0 miles from Par to Truro. On the long grind from Par Harbour up to St Austell, much of it at 1 in 60 speed feel to 21mph and it seemed ironic that with an engine like a 'Castle' at the head of the train the curves on the steeply falling sections west of Burngullow precluded any higher maximum speed than 60mph. Nevertheless we were on time at Truro, 4.06pm, and with the detaching of the Falmouth coach we went forward with the load still further reduced to 335 tons.

After that it was plain sailing so far as the locomotive work was concerned, though in travelling over this part of the line I always recall the remark of a business colleague, asking why this 'star' train passed towns like Redruth and Camborne without stopping, and yet stopped at a place out in the blue like Gwinear Road. It was, of course, a holiday train and the last mentioned stop was to connect with the Helston branch and the holiday districts of the Lizard peninsula. On this trip of mine we shed our last through coach at St Erth, for St Ives, and finished into Penzance, on time, at 5pm with eight coaches. I had noticed on the way down through Cornwall that there seemed to be none save 'Hall' class engines on the local and through services other than our own; and at Ponsondane sheds, once an almost exclusive parade ground for Moguls was now the same for 'Halls', and most of them in none too smart a condition. Having enjoyed the run down I turned my back on the railway for the weekend.

On the Tuesday afterwards I found *Abbotsbury Castle* at the head of the up 'Limited' again with an eight-coach train. We picked up a through coach from St Ives, but a relief train was running ahead of us from Truro, taking sections from Falmouth and Newquay. It cannot have been very far ahead because we were checked by signal approaching Par, and eventually stopped for $3\frac{1}{4}$min outside Plymouth North Road station. Two years later when I was travelling on the same train we had similar trouble with checks from a preceding relief train. Engine No 4094 *Dynevor Castle* with a train heavier by one coach throughout, was stopped by signal outside Truro, checked at St Austell, nearly stopped at Bodmin Road, and checked again at Keyham and outside North Road. The driver of *Abbotsbury Castle* was a little more venturesome in his downhill running, and 'bent the rules' by attaining 69mph descending from Chacewater towards Truro, and 66mph before St Germans. It was all to no avail, because of the signal checks experienced from the relief portion of the train.

At Plymouth, on the two occasions separated by two years, the train was made up to 11 coaches, the tare loads being 360 and 370 tons respectively, and the engines Nos 6007 and 6002, in each case with Old Oak drivers. On the first run with exactly the maximum load for the South Devon line we were unpiloted, but on the second with a load 10 tons over the limit a 'Bulldog' class 4-4-0 No 3401 *Vancouver* was taken as pilot to Hemerdon. Nevertheless although a higher minimum speed was maintained on the bank, 22mph against $17\frac{1}{4}$, the process of slowing down, putting off the pilot, and restarting was so time consuming by comparison that the 'King' that had been assisted up to Hemerdon took 29min to cover the 16.3 miles from North Road to Brent, against $26\frac{3}{4}$min by the engine which had no assistance. And the difference in the gross load was no more than 5 tons! As if to emphasise the comparison, the engine that had taken assistance up to Hemerdon, hurrying to make up the time lost by this 'assistance' made considerably the faster climb from Totnes to Dainton, with a minimum of $27\frac{1}{2}$mph at the summit, against $22\frac{1}{4}$mph. On the non-stop run from Exeter to Paddington 173.5 miles, engine No 6007 *King William III* with the 390-ton train made the journey in $171\frac{1}{2}$min with one signal check, costing 2min. Engine No 6002 *King William IV*, with 395 tons was entirely unchecked, and took exactly 'even time', $173\frac{1}{2}$min, the schedule was then 175min.

Above: Great Western Railway: 4-cylinder 4-6-0 No 4032 *Queen Alexandra*, after rebuilding as a 'Castle', photographed at Ponsondane sheds, Penzance.

Top right: 'Castle' class 4-6-0 No 5079 at Truro. When built, in May 1939 this engine was named *Lydford Castle*, but this was changed to *Lysander* in November 1940. After World War II it was converted to oil firing and worked mainly between Plymouth and Penzance.

Above right: The up 'Cornish Riviera Express' on a summer Saturday preparing to leave Penzance hauled by a 'Bulldog' class 4-4-0 No 3445 *Flamingo* and a mixed traffic 4-6-0 No 5937 *Stanford Hall*.

Right: In the 1930's 'Halls' were the standard motive power on the Cornish main line. Here, No 5915 *Trentham Hall* is at Truro on an up express.

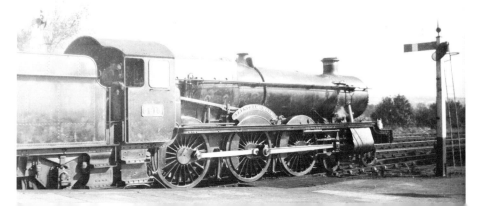

Top: The double-home workings by 'Castles' between Newton Abbot and Shrewsbury on certain west to north services were continued through World War II. In this picture a resplendent No 5032 *Usk Castle* (Salop shed) is heading a very mixed collection of rolling stock, at Exeter, on the 8.45am Plymouth to Liverpool and Manchester.

Above: The first 'King' to have high-degree superheating: No 6022 *King Edward III*, in a postwar picture at Laira shed, before the author rode the engine from Plymouth to Paddington on the up 'Cornish Riviera Express'.

14
Former NBR: Aberdeen-West Highland

The first time I ever saw a North British engine was not ideal, for a genuine appraisal of its elegance. It came on the first journey I made into Scotland, with my parents, during a relatively short wait for a connection at Carlisle. The Atlantic No 880 *Tweeddale* brought in the St Pancras train from Edinburgh. She came under the bridge at the north end into No 2 platform, on which I was standing, and my impression was of a dingy, rather travel stained engine, in a kind of muddy, khaki colour. The traditional 'brown' of North British engines had a distinct olive tinge in it, quite unlike the deep chocolate brown of the Brighton, and it seemed to get more olive-green with age; but this Atlantic had become distinctly 'tatty'. I was not able to study it at leisure, because there came a parental hail from No 1 platform. Our train for Glasgow was just running in. When next I saw North British engines, 'Scotts' and Atlantics alike were resplendent in LNER apple green.

In the ever-welcome Special Scottish Number of *The Railway Magazine*, the late Cecil J. Allen had described in glowing terms the work of the North British Atlantics on the Aberdeen road and in 1928 returning south from the second family holiday at Nairn I had my ticket routed via Aberdeen. The afternoon train from Inverness to the GN of S line connected nicely with the up 'Aberdonian', but by that time third class sleepers had been introduced, and with the train made up to the massive total of 434 tons tare, double heading was essential. We had an Atlantic No 9902 *Highland Chief* leading, and a rebuilt Holmes 4-4-0, No 9769 next to the train. This however, was nothing to the loading I noted on the same train on a later occasion, when an Atlantic and a superheated 'Scott', *Bonnie Dundee* and *Caleb Balderstone*, had no less than 523 tons *tare*, behind them. The ordinary accommodation in the train, apart from the sleepers and the dining car was packed, and the gross load would not have been less than 565 tons. There was a four-wheeled van next to the engines, and it occurred to me to wonder if the draft-gear of that van ever had to transmit such a drawbar pull before.

The remarkable thing about these two runs on the up 'Aberdonian' was the close correspondence of the times, despite the difference in loads. There is no doubt that the two engines on the second run were being worked very hard. I was travelling in the front coach and the continuous roar of the exhausts when climbing the heavy banks was highly significant. A summary of the times is interesting:

The Up 'Aberdeen': Aberdeen-Dundee

Load (tons gross)		470	565
Engines:		Highland Chief	Bonnie Dundee
		No 9769	Caleb Balderstone
	Sch	Time	Time
	min	min sec	min sec
Aberdeen-Stonehaven	24	24 00	23 42
Stonehaven-Montrose	33	32 00	33 40
Montrose-Arbroath	21	20 40	21 15
Arbroath-Dundee	23	22 30	21 05

On the second occasion the 4-wheeler at the front was detached at Dundee and we continued with a 550 ton load. The superheated 'Scott' No 9427 *Lord Glenvarloch* was assistant engine on both trips, and the Atlantics leading were *Liddesdale* and *The Lord Provost*. On the first occasion the schedule for the non-stop run of 59.2 miles to Edinburgh (Waverley) was 83min, but on the second the very severe colliery subsidence slack at Thornton had become operative, right down to 20mph and an extra 2min had been inserted into the schedule to allow for it. This was almost exactly reflected by the longer time taken over this section on the second run. Those taking detailed logs of running over this section often remarked upon the consistency of the point-to-point timekeeping, and these two runs provide an example of this. The following table gives the passing times at the booked schedule points.

Run No			1	2
Load-tons full			470	550
Dist		Sch*	Actual	Actual
Miles		min	min sec	min sec
0.0	Dundee	0	0 00	0 00
2.7	Tay Bridge South	8	7 05	7 05
8.3	Leuchars Jc	14	13 40	13 38
20.1	Ladybank Jc	29	27 35	26 52
28.5	Thornton Jc	39	38 50	38 32
39.1	Burntisland	52	52 20	53 20
46.2	Inverkeithing	62	62 05	63 27
49.7	Dalmeny	69	68 45	71 15
58.0	Haymarket	80	78 20	80 35
—	—	—	check	—
59.2	Waverley	83	82 40	83 55

*Schedule in 1928

Thus, until the Thornton check the two trains were running virtually 'neck and neck', despite the difference in loads, and I can testify again to the 'sound and fury' from the front end when *The Lord Provost* and *Lord Glenvarloch* were climbing the worst banks. The only appreciable difference between the two runs was on the very severe climb from Inverkeithing up to the Forth Bridge, continuously at 1 in 70. *Liddesdale*, and her titled assistant went through Inverkeithing at 45mph against the stipulated 35, and fell only to 28mph on entering upon the Forth Bridge. The *Lord Provost* did not exceed the speed limit by so much, passing Inverkeithing at 40mph, falling afterwards to 23½mph on the bank. In this way the first run gained a complete minute on the second in this short distance.

Between 1928 and 1935 I had many opportunities of seeing the North British Atlantics at work on this route. It was a great sight to see those stationed at Dundee come hammering up on to the cliffs north of Stonehaven. *Aberdonian, Bonnie Dundee, Bon Accord, Thane of Fife* and *Auld Reekie* were ones I well remember. *Highland Chief* was also a favourite, but when the privilege came to me to ride on the footplate it was No 9509 *Duke of Rothesay* that surpassed all. I rode with both her regular drivers, and I place them among the very finest types of steam locomotive enginemen. The elder of the two, John Ogilvy, was then the senior driver at Dundee, to whom there naturally fell various special assignments. When I first met him he was taking over the down 'Aberdonian' before 6am in the chill and darkness of a February morning, and with a load of 401 tons tare he had to take an assistant engine. This latter was one of the non-superheater 'Scotts', No 9340 *Lady of Avenel*. It was always a surprise to me that those 16 original engines of the class were never subsequently superheated, seeing that W. P. Reid began building the superheated version immediately the batch of 10 turned out in 1911 was completed. Of course it is known that superheating costs money, and there were many duties on which the saturated engines could economically be used — main line pilots for one thing. Even in the height of summer it was always interesting to see a double-headed train, with the high superheated Atlantic throwing up a hot, vaporous exhaust, and that from the non-superheated 'Scott' condensing the moment it left the chimney.

This was my first ride on a North British Atlantic, and I was enjoying the easy action of the engine, and the pleasant company of the crew. The conditional stop at Stonehaven was not to be called, and we left Montrose non-stop to Aberdeen. No railway enthusiast can fail to experience a thrill in approaching Kinnaber Junction. Signals were clear for us, although at that time North British trains had to slow to 15mph because of the awkward track layout. But once over the junction we got away in good style, and old John Ogilvy beckoned to me to join him on the left hand side of the engine, and see the Grampians. After a night of snow they hung wrathlike across the sky, exquisitely beautiful in the greyness of a cold winter dawn. While we climbed the Marykirk bank he spoke of the passes leading over to Deeside and of the Royal deer forests around Balmoral; then with mingled pride and modesty he added: 'I've driven the King seven times!'

The Atlantic engine *Duke of Rothesay* was that day working the same roster as that taken up by the 2-8-2 engine *Earl Marischal* later that same year, going north from Dundee a second time on the 3.35pm the 2pm ex-Waverley. With a load of 359 tons tare she was unpiloted, and her second crew, Driver Moodie and Fireman Williamson, gave me a run that is still, after 40 years, one of the classics of my experience on the footplate. There are some who have sought to denigrate the North British Atlantics, partly on the strength of stories of their shortcomings in their early non-superheated days, and of friction over them between the civil and the mechanical engineer; but I would like their detractors to have been with me on the *Duke of Rothesay* that cold February afternoon, and seen the immaculate performance put up by engine and crew. The gross load behind the tender was 380 tons, and it was worked with high efficiency as well as an exhilarating vigour. Moodie was pounding the engine hard on the banks, but she also ran very freely on the level and downhill, and Williamson had plenty of time to talk to me and point out items of interest along the route.

That winter, however, was the beginning of, the end for the North British

Atlantics. The regular working of the first P2 engines, and the drafting of more Pacifics to the route deprived them of their principal duties, and withdrawal of them had already begun. One of them, No 9903 had been named *Cock o' the North*, and when this name was chosen for the first of the P2s the former engine was renamed *Aberdonian*, because the pioneer of the class, No 9868, bearing that name, had already been withdrawn. It was, intended that one of them should have been preserved, and No 9875 *Midlothian* was actually earmarked for this distinction; but three things combined to annul this happy proposal. First of all there was the outbreak of war, in 1939; and then there was the retirement of William Whitelaw from the Chairmanship of the LNER. He was a former North British man, and took much interest in the *personalia* of the locomotive stock. Finally, of course, there was the entry of the iconoclastic Edward Thompson, as successor to Sir Nigel Gresley. Which of the three factors predominated in causing the final withdrawal of *Midlothian* I cannot say.

The other happy hunting ground for lovers of the old North British, and its engines, was the West Highland. I made its acquaintance first from its furthest point in the course of a round trip in Scotland that took me from Glasgow to Inverness, then to Kyle of Lochalsh, and then by steamer to Mallaig. At the time of my first visit, in the autumn of 1932 the line between Fort William and Mallaig was being worked almost entirely by the Reid superheated 0-6-0 goods engines of LNER Class J36. They were the most numerous of all the modern ex-NBR classes and numbered 104 in all; from the viewpoint of traction were very suitable for the Mallaig road. At one time a speed limit of 40mph was imposed throughout between Locheilside and Mallaig, such is the continuous and severe curvature, and a massive 0-6-0 goods engine was ideal for climbing the severe gradients from low initial speed. The passenger trains were not normally heavy.

Between Fort William and Glasgow the 4-4-0s of the 'Glen' series worked nearly all the passenger trains, in pairs when the loads were above the 180-ton maximum permitted to them. They were truly splendid engines, and the way they climbed the banks was exhilarating to record. But when I next visited the West Highland line, and the Mallaig extension, a number of ex-Great Northern 2-cylinder Moguls of Class K2 had been drafted thence. They had a higher tractive effort than the 6ft 'Glen' class 4-4-0s and larger boilers, and they were rated to take a tare load of 220 tons. This did something to reduce the amount of double heading that was necessary with summer loads. Although the rakes of passenger stock were not usually extensive a good deal of fish traffic was conveyed from Mallaig by passenger trains, and very often vans were added to make up the maximum tonnage that could be taken by one engine. A train from Mallaig might have near the maximum for a K2; but if a 'Glen' was rostered for the continuation southward one or two vans would be detached at Fort William and sent forward on the next train.

In logging a number of runs south of Fort William I found that the K2s, although worked very hard, did not make such good speed with their maximum loads of 220 tons as the 'Glens' did with their maximum of 180 tons. It was the kind of country that favoured engines fitted with the Stephenson link motion, and its characteristic of varying lead, with cut-off. I believe that Cowlairs works made some small changes to the K2 engines that were allocated to the West Highland to strengthen up their performance at low speed on the heaviest banks. They were nearly all named after lochs lying on or near the route, and were all kept in beautiful condition. They were not such comfortable engines to ride as the 'Glens'. Their cabs were like those of the Great Northern Atlantics with lever reverse on the right hand side. The visitor was usually given a small wooden seat on the left side, so high that it left one's legs dangling. I used to steady myself against the rocking and vibrating of the engine by bracing one foot against a protruding bolt on the firebox front.

The 'Glens' were lovely engines to ride. They had left hand drive, and they ran very freely, and after the lapse of years I can tell that they frequently, and regularly exceeded the maximum speed limits laid down for the line. I have recorded speeds up to 64mph with them, and at such speeds, I may add, they still rode very smoothly. In the 1930s engines and their crews were working through between Glasgow and Fort William, and the 'Glens' used to make merry on the level stretches beside the Firth of Clyde, east of Craigendoran. The very popular Sunday excursions from Glasgow to Fort William and Mallaig were usually worked by a pair of 'Glens'. Their load limit enabled these trains to be made up to 360 tons tare, and as time went on the demand for accommodation became such that the trains had to be duplicated. Then the main train was made up to 400 tons tare, maximum for a K2 and a 'Glen', and the relief portion up to the maximum for a K2. There was always great animation on the waterfront at Fort William on arrival of these trains. Not all passengers elected to make the journey through to Mallaig, or other stations on the extension line, and normally the relief train did not run beyond Fort William. In the confined space, and short platform lengths it needed careful organisation to avoid getting operations tangled up. But North British operation between the wars was usually very good, and these long and heavy excursion trains ran punctually in my experience.

Nevertheless, the amount of double heading necessary in the summer holiday season was not to Gresley's liking. Unfortunately the limitation upon maximum axle loading imposed by the West Highland viaducts precluded any spectacular solution of the problem such as the introduction of the P2 engines on the Aberdeen road. The Garratt type of locomotive would have provided a solution, but one of the abiding difficulties of a line like the West Highland was that for nine months in the year the loads did not demand anything larger than a K2, and a giant engine that would work the Sunday excursions, and the Kings Cross 'sleepers' in the tourist season would be very much under-utilised, and extravagant in consequence. Gresley's palliative — one could not call it a complete solution — was to design a 3-cylinder Mogul that would come within the maximum axle-load limitations, but by having the improved steam distribution of the standard front end have a more economical performance than a K2 and enable a much higher nominal tractive effort to be built in.

The resulting K4 class was a very interesting compromise. Gresley would obviously have liked the put the K3 boiler on to an engine of such high tractive effort, but the weight would have been excessive for the West Highland. The significant dimensions of the three classes were:

LNER 2-6-0 Designs

Class	K2	K3	K4
Cylinders number	2	3	3
dia (in)	20	$18\frac{1}{2}$	$18\frac{1}{2}$
stroke (in)	26	26	26
Coupled wheel dia (ft-in)	5-8	5-8	5-2
Total combined heating surface (sq ft)	1,984	2,308	1,732
Boiler pressure (psi)	170	180	200
Adhesion wt (tons)	53.4	60.85	57.8
Nom tractive effort (ft)	22,070	30,031	36,600

The K4 was thus very powerful, but its boiler would not sustain a big effort for very long. I rode the pioneer engine No 3441 *Loch Long*, and she handled a train of 286 tons tare very competently. The load limit for the class was fixed at 300 tons and five more engines were built at Darlington in 1938-9. I saw them at work in 1939, but it was not until after World War II that I had any runs with engines Nos 3442-3446.

Technicalities apart I have always felt that there is nothing to compare with the West Highland line anywhere else in Great Britain. It has interests for everyone to a superlative degree. To engineers of all disciplines there are fields of evergreen interest, in the maintenance of the line and its structures, in a wild, remote, and often harsh countryside, while I have already shown how its haulage problems were tackled by Sir Nigel Gresley. To the railway enthusiast the subjects for photographs and lineside study are limitless, while its setting, in some of most varied and majestic scenery in the West Highlands, gives it an appeal to lovers of wild nature — railway or not. Then again it is steeped in Scottish history Glen Falloch; a sight of the mountains of Glencore; Inverlochy, Fassifern, Glen Finnan and Loch nan Uamh all stir the blood. To ride one of the trains, and listen to the sharp staccato exhaust of *Glen Dochart, Loch Morar*, or just at the end of our period, perhaps, *The Great Marquess* was to experience a journey without parallel.

Above: The magnificent North British Atlantics: No 9872 *Auld Reekie*, at Stonehaven on the down 'Night Scotsman', assisted by a non-superheated 'Scott' class 4-4-0 No 9899 *Jeanie Deans.*

Top right: One of the superheated 'Scotts' No 9424 *Lady Rowena*, at Tweedmouth Junction shed in 1933.

Above right: Down goods train north of Stonehaven hauled by ex-North British superheater 0-6-0 No 9477 (LNER Class J37).

Right: Edinburgh-Aberdeen express, with, next to the engines, through carriage for Elgin, climbing on to the cliffs north of Stonehaven, hauled by 4-4-2 No 9868 *Aberdonian* and 'Scott' class 4-4-0 No 9899 *Jeanie Deans.*

Top left: Edinburgh-Aberdeen express just after leaving Leuchars Junction hauled by 4-4-2 locomotive No 9510 *The Lord Provost.*

Above left: An ex-NBR superheated 4-4-2T of 1915 design (LNER Class C16), No 9445, at Leuchars Junction in 1935.

Left: Edinburgh express with through carriages for Kings Cross, leaving Aberdeen hauled by 4-4-2 No 9509 *Duke of Rothesay* and superheated 'Scott' class 4-4-0 No 9423 *Quentin Durward.*

Top: On the West Highland line: Mallaig-Glasgow express at Crianlarich, hauled by 4-4-0 locomotives Nos 9406 *Glen Croe* and 9494 *Glen Loy.* Note the two water columns, so that engines of a double headed train could be watered simultaneously.

Above: The small locomotive yard at Mallaig, with ex-NBR Class J37 0-6-0 No 9044, and a highly burnished K2 2-6-0 No 4691 *Loch Morar*

Top: Glasgow express preparing to leave Fort William, hauled by 4-4-0 locomotive No 9100 *Glen Dochart*

Above: Express for the south leaving Fort William headed by 2-6-0 No 4691 *Loch Morar*, and 4-4-0 No 9494 *Glen Loy.*

15
Great Northern and Great Southern of Ireland

Just before Whitsun 1936 I crossed from Liverpool to Dublin in one of the elderly, but very comfortable steam turbine ships of the British and Irish Steam Packet Company. It was my first visit to Eire, and the grass green funnels of the *Lady Leinster* were an added reminder of where we were going. Next morning I was riding the engine of the morning express through to Belfast however, and at Amiens Street I found our engine decked in the nearest approach to 'Caledonian blue' I had seen since 1923. It was one of the Glover 3-cylinder compounds based very closely on the Midland design, but that blue livery was a startling departure in more than one way. Consciously, or unconsciously the leading Irish railways in earlier days had tended to model their practice on one or another of the English companies, and just as I shall tell later the Great Southern and Western formed quite a strong affinity to the London and North Western, so the Great Northern inclined quite strongly towards the English Great Northern.

When Charles Clifford was Locomotive Superintendent the engines were painted in a style almost exactly following that of Doncaster, with the initials GNR on the tenders, in transfer letters, and it was only the names, and the coat of arms that gave some indication of the difference. When Glover succeeded Clifford his first engines were painted in the same style but early in World War I he changed to plain black, and his compounds, when they first came out, in 1932 were in the same undistinguished livery. The decision to paint this one small class of express passenger engine in a style entirely new to Ireland, bright blue, with crimson underframes, set a precedent, if not in actual livery but certainly in practice, that was later followed by the LNER with their ever-celebrated A4 Pacifics. As I shall tell in the next chapter there were several reasons for doing this, but the Great Northern of Ireland got in first.

I gathered however, that the Glover compounds were not as generally popular with their drivers as their bright paint would suggest. At Amiens Street that morning when I presented my credentials to the driver I was greeted by one of those Irishisms that can baffle an unsuspecting stranger. But I was reassured; and there was more than a twinkle in his roguish eye when he said: 'You're from over the water', and when I nodded assent he thundered' 'I wish you fellers would stay in HELL and leave us in peace!' And then I was ushered aboard, and made as welcome as on any other footplate, anywhere in the world. He made no secret of that fact that he didn't think much of the compounds. In traction matters the depths of denigration are sometimes equated to the drawbar pull necessary to detach the skin from a rice pudding; but old Bob Batten averred that his compound wouldn't pull a broody hen off its nest! — and then, of course, to complete the Irishism, gave me an excellent run to Dundalk, to the accompaniment of continuous badinage from his side of the footplate. I don't think I have ever laughed so much on an engine, and when he was relieved by a Dundalk driver for the continuation run to Belfast he gripped my hand as in a vice saying: 'The height of good luck to ye!.'

Rather more than two years later I met Batten again in the course of a very hectic 36 hours of railway notetaking. The Great Northern Railway were then in process of renewing the eight superheated 4-4-0s of Glover's 1913 design. I have no doubt that accountancy-wise this job would be classed as a 'rebuild', but with new and deeper frames, new cylinders, and new boilers there was not a great deal of the original engines left. The first to be modernised, and painted blue No 173 *Galteemore*, was completed at Dundalk in May 1938, and No 192 *Slieve-na-Mon* followed a month later. From friends 'across the water' I had learned of their excellent performance, and although on reflection, it was a trifle venturesome weather-wise to make a weekend trip to Ireland in December it turned out that I was very lucky. I had a smooth crossing on the mail packet from Holyhead on the Friday night, and was round at Amiens Street next morning in time to footplate the 6.40am 'Limited Mail', once again with Bob Batten, and this time on *Galteemore*. 'Och, its yerself', he exclaimed 'Now ye've come to ride on a *locomotive!*' 'She's good is she?' I asked: 'Splendid' — and in his tremendous emphasis of the word came a wealth of enthusiasm.

In addition to the structural improvements and higher boiler pressure there were some changes to the Stephenson link motion; and although the compounds were fast engines, attaining speeds up to 85mph much more readily that their English counterparts they could not hold a candle to *Galteemore* and her kind, that used to dash up to 90mph with no more than the slightest encouragement. The down morning mail was then allowed 33min to cover the 31.7 miles from Dublin to Drogheda, and then 25min for the ensuing 22.6 miles on to Dundalk, in both cases start to stop. In the latter case it begins with a continuous climb of nearly 5 miles at 1 in 177 up to Kellystown box. With a train of 240 tons, *Galteemore* and her crew made the job look easy, keeping time, save for a few seconds, to Drogheda, despite a long permanent way slowing, and gaining nearly a minute to Dundalk. At speeds between 77 and 82mph the engine rode beautifully, though of course the 5ft 3in gauge would be an advantage in this respect.

On my visit in 1936 I spent the Whitsun weekend in the neighbourhood of Dundalk, and took many photographs of trains in the hilly country between there and the other 'border' station of Goraghwood. At that time all engines except the compounds were painted black, though smartly turned out and unnamed. There were only five of the compounds, and they could not cover all the express workings between Dublin and Belfast. Their introduction recalled that of the simple superheater 4-4-0s in 1913, in that only five of them were built in the first place, and all named. These names were all revived when the engines were renewed in 1938-9. They are interesting to set beside those of the compounds, both Glover designs yet separated by 19 years.

GNR (I) 4-4-0s

1913 Simples		1932 Compounds	
No 170	*Errigal*	No 83	*Eagle*
No 171	*Slieve Gullion*	No 84	*Falcon*
No 172	*Slieve Donard*	No 85	*Merlin*
No 173	*Galteemore*	No 86	*Peregrine*
No 174	*Carrantuohill*	No 87	*Kestrel*

Three more of the superheater 4-4-0s were added in 1917, Nos 190-192 but these did not originally bear names. Fine titles of mountains in the west were found for them when they were renewed in 1938-9. Even before their renewal however these veteran 4-4-0s were capable of excellent work, and I remember being positively shaken by the speed at which No 190, then in black, came tearing down the bank from Adavoyle to Dundalk, one day when I was photographing up in the hills. It was there that I was later to clock up a maximum speed of $86\frac{1}{2}$mph with the renewed No 173 *Galteemore*, on the up mail, on that hectic December round of which I wrote earlier. To assuage the curiosity of my readers the complete itinerary was:

6pm Euston to Wilmslow
9.58pm Wilmslow back to Crewe
12.8am Crewe to Holyhead (arr 2.25am)
6.10am Kingstown Pier to Dublin
6.40am Dublin to Belfast
A day on the NCC including a trip to Portrush and back
5.40pm Belfast to Dublin
The connection to Kingstown Pier and thence to Holyhead
12.13am Holyhead to Chester, after which I gave up timing!

The 6.10am from Kingstown Pier was a through breakfast car express to Belfast, which, with an arrival at 9.10am, gave a faster service from Euston to Belfast than by the Stranraer-Larne route. The respective times were then:

	Euston dep	Belfast arr
Via Holyhead-Kingstown	8.45pm	9.10am
Via Stranraer-Larne	7.40pm	8.58am

The overall time of $2\frac{1}{2}$ hours from Dublin to Belfast was excellent in view of the customs examinations at both Dundalk and Goraghwood. The booked running times for the 107.7 miles totalled up to no more than 115min, an average of 56mph.

My first journeys on the Great Southern came in the early summer, and began with a through trip from London to Cork. As with the mail train services on the Great Northern, and those of the former Midland and Great Western lines, the timing of what were then referred to as the 'English Mails' between Dublin and Cork was arranged to connect with the sailings of the Irish Mail steamers between Holyhead and Kingstown Pier. I believe that at one time the postal service in Ireland was such that a letter posted in time to catch the down 'Irish Mail' could expect a reply by return of post from places as far distant as Cork or Galway. The turn-round times at those two cities were then 4hr 55min, and 4hr 30min respectively! Whether any one ever attempted it is another matter. So far as the Great Southern was concerned the connection left Kingstown Pier at 6.10am and the mail train left Kingsbridge at 7am. It detached coaches at Kildare and Maryborough, but whether these were through vehicles for the Kilkenny and Waterford branches I cannot remember.

The immediate start out of Dublin (Kingsbridge) is severe with $1\frac{1}{2}$ miles at 1 in 117-84 to Inchicore, and on my first journey a load of 11 coaches, 323 tons tare, was enough for one of the 2-cylinder 4-6-0s, then fitted with Caprotti valve gear, to be piloted by a 4-4-0 engine No 328. The assistant engine was taken only as far as Kildare, at which place the load was reduced to 301 tons, or 320 with passengers and luggage. Those Great Southern 4-6-0s had had a chequered history. When R. E. L. Maunsell left Ireland in 1913 to become Chief Mechanical Engineer of the South Eastern and Chatham Railway he was succeeded at Inchicore by his works manager, E. A. Watson, an ex-GWR man and a fervent disciple of Churchward. He had been a little too fervent at times for Maunsell's liking, who once exclaimed 'Mr Watson thinks all Swindon geese are swans!'. It can, however, be recalled that when Maunsell had the task of building up his new team on the SE&CR most of them came from Swindon! Anyway Watson's first express passenger design was a 4-cylinder 4-6-0 for which much of the inspiration came from the Great Western 'Star'. Only one engine was built at first, No 400, but then, in 1920, construction of nine more was authorised. Three, Nos 401, 402 and 406 were built at Inchicore, and the other six were ordered from Armstrong Whitworth & Co. It was rather extraordinary that three of the latter were built non-superheated, and using a boiler pressure of 225lb sq in instead of the 175 on No 400, and its superheated successors.

To say that these 4-cylinder 4-6-0s were not entirely satisfactory is to flatter the design. Although reputed to be powerful and fast, they were constantly in trouble, and were heavy on coal and water. Watson's successor, J. R. Bazin from the Great Northern, of England, had to take drastic measures. In 1927 he rebuilt No 402 as a two-cylinder machine, with a completely new chassis and wheels, as well as cylinders and motion; and there being less need for large engines in the economic circumstances of the time the pioneer engine, No 400, was scrapped outright in 1929, followed by Nos 404 and 408 in the following year. Then Nos 401 and 406 were rebuilt in a similar way to No 402, but fitted with the Beardmore-Caprotti valve gear. These engines also had new frames, and little of the originals remained, except for the boilers. The remaining four engines Nos 403, 405, 407 and 409 were also rebuilt, but using the original frames strengthened and modified only at the front end. This greatly reduced the cost of rebuilding. When I made my first journeys on the Great Southern these seven 4-6-0s were holding down the main line work, except at the two ends of the line.

I found No 401 a nice engine to ride, except that I was surprised to see the driver never link her up below 30% and work for the most part on the first valve of the regulator. This seemed to me the absolute negation of all the advantages claimed for poppet valve-gear, though no comment came from Inchicore when I sent them the draft of the reports I wrote. The engine ran very freely and we kept good time throughout. Some time afterwards I had some correspondence with the manufacturers of the valve-gear, and I learned that considerable trouble had been experienced by them in trying to get the drivers to link right up and keep the regulator full open. One of their engineers wrote to me:

'I first travelled on engine No 401 in 1938 and found that owing to the handwheel only having cut-off positions indicated up to 10% they had never known that it was possible to notch up as far as 3%. In fact many of the drivers said that I was putting her in reverse when I tried to show what could be done in that direction. I made the additional markings for 7, 5 and 3% and although we did remarkably good work in 1939 with full regulator and short cut-offs the drivers have a very strong inclination for half regulator and 20% working even now!'

Of course in 1939 all attention at Inchicore was centred upon the introduction of Edgar Bredin's beautiful 3-cylinder 4-6-0 *Maeve* and no one in high authority would be particularly interested in the working of the two Caprotti engines.

Apart from new main line engines, Cork, Glanmire sheds were a positive treasure trove for lovers of historic locomotives. Just imagine a place where, in the later 1930s, one could see engines designed by McDonnell, H. A. Ivatt, Coey, Watson, R. E. L. Maunsell and Bazin, in the same yard at the same time! The somewhat ancient 0-6-0 goods had all received new boilers, but their chassis and machinery dated back to McDonnell, before he left Inchicore for his brief and ill-starred stay on the North Eastern at Gateshead. H. A. Ivatt, later of Doncaster fame, was represented by one of the handsome little 4-4-2Ts built in 1894, for the long branch lines running westward to Kenmare and Valentia Harbour. There were also several of Ivatt's 0-6-0Ts on shed. Robert Coey was represented by 4-4-0s of the 300 series, used as main line pilots, and for some semi-fast trains. There was also an ex-Midland and Great Western 4-4-0 of the 'Kylemore' class, still easily recognisable from its distinctively shaped dome cover, and the curious jutting-out smokebox front. Like all the former GS&W engines it was painted dark grey, devoid of any lining, but having the Crewe-type cast number plates on the cab sides. Before the amalgamation of 1925 the MGW engines in dark blue with red lining, were some of the most attractive looking in Ireland.

R. E. L. Maunsell would undoubtedly have been gratified to see engines of his SE&CR 2-6-0 design at Glanmire sheds. The GS&WR purchased a number of those built at Woolwich Arsenal, and converted them to the 5ft 3in. There were two of them on shed at the time of my first visit to Cork. By the time of my second visit however Mr Bredin had rebuilt two of the 400 class express passenger 4-6-0s with larger boilers, and I saw and photographed No 403; but at that time all attention, so far as main line express engines were concerned, was concentrated upon *Maeve*, and in her handsome green livery she did present a glittering spectacle, among the grey, unlined engines of all vintages that stood on the shed roads around her: a large-boilered 400; two ex-MGW 4-4-0s; a McDonnell 0-6-0, and two Ivatt 0-6-0Ts! I have no record of what engines were inside the shed; those just mentioned were all outside.

The afternoon's event at Cork was the departure of the 'English Mail'. At the time of my first visit this was at 3.50pm. It was usually a heavy train and assistance was essential up the terrific incline that began immediately beyond the platform end. At once one dived into a tunnel nearly a mile long on gradients of 1 in 78-64, and then on emerging, after no more than a momentary respite, there came all but 2 miles at 1 in 60. There was a good deal more in it that just providing tractive assistance. To hammer a way up such a bank at the very start of a three-hour journey was enough to knock the heart of the most carefully prepared firebed to pieces; and if, by the provision of assistance, the train engine could be worked less than 'all-out' during those first few minutes it was all to the good. On my first up journey the Caprotti 4-6-0 No 401, with a load of 390 tons, had a 4-4-0 as pilot to Ballybrophy, and these two engines would normally have been able to mount the initial bank; but to avoid their having to be unduly exerted in the first 10 minutes, a third engine was coupled ahead — one of the old 0-6-0s, which assisted as far as Blarney. The three engines sustained 24mph up the 1 in 60, and reached Blarney, 5.8 miles, in just under the 14min scheduled.

In view of this experience it can well be imagined with what anticipation, indeed with what excitement I learned that in August 1939, when the mail was loaded up to 421 tons tare, *Maeve* was going to tackle this big train without any assistance at all: three engines previously for 390 tons, but now the one new engine was going to take 450 tons on her own. I was not the only one down at Glanmire sheds who was excited at the prospect. The District Locomotive Superintendent, the senior locomotive inspector, and the shedmaster all decided to join us on the footplate, so that with a headquarters inspector from Inchicore and the driver and fireman there were seven of us, as far as Mallow. That initial bank was mounted in gallant style, with a sustained speed of $22\frac{1}{2}$mph on the 1 in 60; but the terrific hammering involved disturbed the firebed, and although we had passed Blarney in $14\frac{1}{2}$min, we were troubled with indifferent steaming for the next hour of the run to Dublin. With the outbreak of war only three weeks later news of *Maeve's* continuing prowess ceased to come across the water.

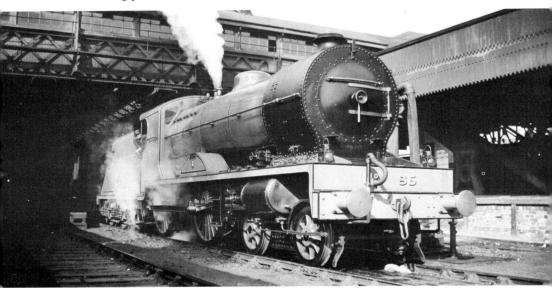

Left: Great Northern Railway (Ireland): one of the Glover 3-cylinder compound 4-4-0s No 85 *Merlin*, on express for Belfast at Amiens Street station, Dublin. This photograph shows off the sky-blue livery adopted for these engines in 1936.

Below left: GNR(I) one of the small 4-4-0s as rebuilt, No 46, seen here at Goraghwood, junction for the Warrenpoint line.

Above: GNR(I) superheater 4-4-0 No 173 *Galteemore* as renewed in 1938, and painted in the blue livery originally applied only to the compounds.

Below: Great Southern: one of the Watson 4-6-0s of the GS&WR as rebuilt with 2-cylinders and Caprotti valve-gear; photographed at Cork after the author had ridden this engine from Dublin.

Top left: GSR 4-4-0 No 305, of the second series introduced by R. Coey in 1902. The engine is shown here as rebuilt, and working from Cork, Glanmire shed in 1937.

Above left: A GS&WR veteran at Cork in 1937. Engine No 37 4-4-2T, was built by H. A. Ivatt in 1894 for working on the long branch lines to Kenmare and Valentia Harbour. The 'D' shaped smokebox was introduced when the engine was rebuilt.

Left: Cork, in 1939: a semi-fast train ready to leave for Dublin, headed by 0-6-0 No 176 and a 4-4-0 of the 300 class.

Top: One of the 4-cylinder 4-6-0s of Watson's designs, as rebuilt with two cylinders, and larger boiler, No 402 at Cork in 1939.

Above: An ex-Midland & Great Western 4-4-0, No 546, of the 'Kylemore' class, having a distinctive appearance, in contrast to the ex-GS&W engines of Coey design: photographed at Cork in 1939.

Top: Cork, Glanmire shed in 1939: engines left to right are a McDonnell standard 0-6-0 goods No 131; an ex-MGW 4-4-0; the new 3-cylinder 4-6-0 No 800 *Maeve* being polished up ready to work the 'English Mail', and an old 0-6-0T shunting engine.

Above: E. C. Bredin's beautiful 3-cylinder 4-6-0 No 800 *Maeve*, at Cork, preparatory to working the 'English Mail', on which the author rode on the footplate.

162

16
High Speed — LNER and LMS

I must admit to having mixed feelings the first time I saw *Silver Link* at Kings Cross. The date was 27 September 1935 — 110 years to the very day from the opening of the Stockton and Darlington Railway. I am by nature a traditionalist in all the various walks of life down which I have ventured, and *Silver Link* was a shattering blow to some of those long cherished sentiments as to what a British locomotive should look like. Gresley had to some extent prepared us for the unconventional in the 'hush-hush' No 10000 and in *Cock o' the North*; but *Silver Link* thrust the unconventional in locomotive lineaments much farther forwards. And there was colour, too! It was a time when streamlining was a catch-word, to be applied indiscriminately to tooth-brushes, domestic kettles, and to the exterior of signalboxes! And *Silver Link* caught popular fancy with a vengeance, and created a sensation; she was certainly meant to do so.

We learned afterwards that a great deal of deep thinking lay behind the evolution of that unusually shaped front-end. The cynics who said it was a mere pandering to popular taste added more than a grain of truth when they said it was not true streamlining at all, and that the front should have been smoothed and rounded in every plane. Actually it was a most ingenious and efficacious compromise. The largest LNER express locomotives had, with one solitary exception been free of the troubles experienced on the LMS and the Southern with steam beating down and obscuring the driver's lookout. The one exception had been the piston-valve P2 No 2002 *Earl Marischal*, which had been cured by the addition of the ugly deflector screens. It was obvious that a locomotive with a streamlined front, and no projections above the line of the boiler would be particularly susceptible to exhaust steam clinging to the outside of the boiler. Gresley however, with his wide knowledge of, and close interest in French railway practice had noted the wedge-shaped fronts of the high speed Bugatti railcars, and the front end of the new LNER Pacifics was modelled on these, but with the flat surface curving backwards. It proved outstandingly successful in deflecting the exhaust steam high over the cab, even when the engine was steaming very lightly. Experiments made at the National Physical Laboratory in a wind tunnel, comparing the front-end shapes of the A3 and A4 Pacifics showed that approximately 135hp was saved by the reduction of head-on air resistance at 90mph.

If her static appearance was sensational the first public outing of *Silver Link* on that ever memorable 27 September 1935 was no less so. For on the Invitation Run, for distinguished guests and representatives of the Press, the engine not only achieved a maximum speed of $112\frac{1}{2}$mph but sustained an average speed of 100mph for 43 miles on end. Not for the first time in British railway history however, locomotive engineering technology, in providing motive power, had moved far ahead of the vitally associated arts of signalling and brake power. It was not that technology in these latter spheres *could* not produce equipment and installations to match the advances in locomotive practice; they had not been called upon to do so. It was ironical too that the one section of line between Kings Cross and Newcastle with the most modern signalling equipment, that between York and Northallerton, provided the most restrictive conditions towards the running of the 'Silver Jubilee' express.

The basic speed of the new streamlined flyer on level track was to be 90mph and on the York-Northallerton section, equipped with 3-aspect colour light signals throughout the spacing between successive signals was about 1,200yd. On the 'Silver Jubilee', originally fitted with the ordinary vacuum brake, there was not sufficient distance between successive signals to stop, from a full 90mph when making a full service application. Of course in most conditions of visibility a driver would receive a sight of a yellow signal some considerable distance before he came up level with it, and would brake accordingly; but it was essential to have full braking distance between signals, and so on this stretch, otherwise ideal for very fast running, the 'Jubilee' was limited to a maximum speed of 70mph. South of York, with mechanical signalling throughout, the train was 'double-blocked' — in other words two block sections ahead were required to be clear before the starting signals could be lowered. The signalling between York and Northallerton was in due course changed to 4-aspect, and experiments were in progress up to the outbreak of war in 1939 with an improved form of vacuum brake. Of course much better retardation would have been obtained had air brakes then been standard; but that is another story.

In the Silver Jubilee year of 1935 no such colateral development towards considerably higher speeds had yet begun on the LMS. The policy of that company, as more of the Stanier standard locomotives became available, was towards a steady acceleration of all its main line services, even including those most heavily loaded. The experience with the first two Pacific engines Nos 6200 and 6201 had led to important changes in boiler design, and some very hard test runs with the former engine made in June 1935 showed that the original failings, due to inadequate degree of superheat, had been eradicated. During that same summer 10 more Pacifics with the improved boiler were built at Crewe. I had the privilege of visiting the works at that time and saw Nos 6208, 6209 and 6210 at varying stages of completion. They proved magnificent engines in traffic, and their success made possible the notable accelerations of the 'Midday Scot', in 1936. It was the insertion of a stop at Penrith, with a start-to-stop allowance of 59min for the 51.2miles from Lancaster that made maximum demands on the locomotives in the course of through workings from Euston to Glasgow. It is one of my regrets that I was never able to manage a trip on the down train, with which time was kept with loads up to 530 tons; but I had one remarkable run with the up train, with a load of no less than 570 tons, on which Shap Summit 31.4 miles, was passed in 42½min from the Carlisle start, and despite a permanent way check south of Oxenholme, Carnforth, 62.8miles, was passed in 71min, 3min, early, and Lancaster was reached in 77½min. The engine was No 6206 *Princess Marie Louise*.

By the summer of 1936 it was becoming generally known in railway circles that the LNER was planning a second high speed streamlined service for Coronation Year, this time from Kings Cross to Edinburgh. It had been all very well for the LMS to stand aside while their friendly rivals were running a very fast, but quite non-competitive service to Newcastle. It was another matter, when the high-speed enterprise was extended into Scotland. Although LMS interests in Edinburgh were not so strong as those in Glasgow, in face of this new development they could hardly stand aside. By the late autumn of 1936 the LNER were planning a 6-hour service between Kings Cross and Edinburgh, 392.7 miles. This would involve an overall average speed of 65.4mph, but if a similar overall time was to be made between Euston and Glasgow, the average speed over the longer distance of 401.4 miles including the ascents to Shap and Beattock summits, would be 66.9mph. The answer to this challenge was to try it out, and at mid-November with engine No 6201 *Princess Elizabeth* and a load of 225 tons — roughly the same as that of the LNER 'Silver Jubilee' train — the 401.4 mile trip was made non-stop in 6¼min inside the level 6 hours. On the return journey on the following day, with an extra coach, a considerably faster time of 5hr 44¼min was made — a remarkable average of 70.15mph.

At the time much was made of the fact that this truly splendid performance had been made by a standard, non-streamlined locomotive, though of course it could equally be recalled that a very fast test run, with a standard Pacific engine *Papyrus* and coaches had been made on the LNER from Newcastle to Kings Cross in March 1935 when the 'Silver Jubilee' timing was anticipated and bettered by more than 10min. The 'Jubilee' had a booked average of 70mph over the 232 miles between Kings Cross and Darlington, but that it did not always need such highly sophisticated Pacific engines to make such averages, with a train of 230 tons, was amusingly shown by a run of my own on the so-called 'Liverpool Flyer', 6.12pm from Crewe to Willesden Junction. The booked time for that 152.7 miles was then 142min. No Pacific or 'Royal Scot' was available that evening and a load of 415 tons was entrusted to two 5X 4-6-0s, a 'Baby Scot' No 5524 *Sir Frederick Harrison*, leading, and a Stanier 'Jubilee', No 5673 then unnamed. In making up time from various checks their net time was 126½min, an average from start to stop of 72.4mph and 99 miles in the aggregate were run at an average speed of 80mph. Furthermore the maximum only once reached as much as 90mph.

This amounts to suggesting that a 'Baby Scot' or a Stanier 5X in first class condition could have run the 'Silver Jubilee' on the LNER. With expert drivers and first class coal they probably could have done; but there would have been very little margin, even when all the circumstances were favourable. It was the experiment of making these two very strenuous non-stop runs between Euston and Glasgow that suggested to the Locomotive Department of the LMS that even the 'Princess Royal' class Pacifics were not ideal for such an assignment, particularly as a rather heavier load than that of the 'Silver Jubilee' was contemplated. I think all LMS supporters were very disappointed when it was announced that the 'Coronation Scot' train, to be introduced in the summer of 1937, would take 6½hrs from Euston to Glasgow, inclusive of one stop, at Carlisle. Nevertheless, while it had been shown how brilliantly the Stanier Pacifics could perform, I have always thought that the 6½hr schedule was intended only as a beginning, and that as the men got used to the continuous fast running, over the long Euston-Carlisle non-stop runs it would be possible to accelerate. As it was, apart from that hectic Invitation Run of 29 June 1937 the 'Coronation Scot' offered little interest to the compiler of train-running logs.

The introduction of Pacifics on to the Euston-Liverpool trains gave me some excellent runs, and very clearly showed the big advantage these engines had over the 'Royal Scots' with maximum load trains. Towards the end of my period the streamlined 'Coronation' class engines began to appear on these workings, and they in turn displayed an equally big advance over the 'Lizzies', as the 'Princess Royal' class 4-6-2s were becoming affectionately known. We used to get the 'Turbomotive' No 6202, on the down 'Merseyside Express', and brief reference to some of these runs are interesting as showing the kind of work that was being done regularly by these big engines.

The Merseyside Express 4-6-2 Engines
Euston to Crewe, 158.1 miles

Engine No	Name	Load tons gross	Net time passing Crewe	Maximum speed mph
6212	Duchess of Kent	505	159	$80\frac{1}{2}$
6204	Princess Louise	500	$162\frac{3}{4}$*	$77\frac{1}{2}$
6202	'Turbomotive'	515	159	82
6211	Queen Maud	535	155	$80\frac{1}{2}$
6229	Duchess of Hamilton	520	$152\frac{1}{2}$	79

*No checks: actual time, passing $1\frac{1}{4}$min early

I had another very fast up journey on which No 6228 *Duchess of Rutland* made a net time of $151\frac{1}{2}$min from Crewe to Euston with a load of 490 tons with a twice repeated maximum of 85mph. Of the down runs, the first, second and fourth were punctual on arrival in Liverpool; the third was delayed by fog after Crewe, and the fifth, on a very snowy night, was $2\frac{3}{4}$min late passing Crewe, but after further checks, 6min late on arrival at Lime Street. It will be appreciated that average speeds of 60mph and over, were the order of the day with loads of 500 tons, plus.

From 1937 onwards with the introduction of the 'Coronation' streamliner, the LNER was stealing most of the show from the viewpoint of speed. Furthermore, the 'Coronation' was a much harder locomotive assignment than the 'Silver Jubilee'. Not only was the load some 40% heavier, but one engine worked through between Kings Cross and Edinburgh, remained at York going north, and Newcastle southbound. To crown all, the start-to-stop run of 157min from Kings Cross to York by the down train snatched, by a few decimal points, the honour of running the fastest train in the British Empire from the Great Western — 71.9mph against the 71.4mph of the 'Cheltenham Flyer'. Again, there was no comparison for difficulty between the two runs, quite apart from the LNER engine having to make the trip as the first stage of a 392.7 mile through working. In view of the difficulties that developed in running the 'Coronation' during the winter storms even when the load was reduced by omitting the observation car, I was always a little surprised that engines were not changed at Newcastle. At the start of the service, of course, this could not be done, because the down train ran non-stop from York to Edinburgh; but a stop at Newcastle was inserted later, while maintaining the overall time of 6hrs from Kings Cross.

With the full 9-coach load, weighing 312 tons tare it needed some hard work to keep time, especially if there was an awkward cross-wind. Streamlining gave no help in such conditions. At that time there were speed restrictions to 15mph through Peterborough, 60 at Retford, 60 at Doncaster, and usually about 30mph through Selby. One noticed also the effect of the 'cold' start from Kings Cross on the down journey. On one particular run, of first rate quality, one noticed that whereas speed fell from an initial 65mph through Wood Green to 55mph at the summit of the long 1 in 200 to Potters Bar, later in the same journey when the engine was thoroughly warmed up a speed of 76mph was sustained up the same inclination from Little Bytham to Corby. On this journey, with engine No 4490 *Empire of India*, a total of 154 miles, from Brookmans Park to Fletton Junction, and then from Werrington Junction to Brayton Junction, were covered at an average speed of 79mph and this included slacks to 60mph over water troughs at Langley Junction and Newark, and slacks to 62mph at Retford, and 59mph through Doncaster. The maximum speed attained was 95mph.

I had an enjoyable run on the southbound train, through from Edinburgh to Kings Cross in August 1937, with engine No 4491 *Commonwealth of Australia*. It did not need any exceptionally fast running to cover the initial 57.5miles to Berwick in $54\frac{3}{4}$min, and we clocked into Newcastle, 124.4 miles, in $118\frac{3}{4}$min, $1\frac{1}{4}$min early; but having remanned the engine even the apparently generous 40min allowed for the first 36 miles to passing Darlington were insufficient by $2\frac{1}{2}$min because of three slowings through areas of colliery subsidence, involving reductions to within 20 and 30mph. Then came that tantalising section from Northallerton to York where we could have got away in earnest, but limited to 70mph because of the signal spacing.

Our driver slightly 'bent the rules' by averaging 73.2mph from Northallerton to Poppleton Junction (now Skelton) and the train was no more than 45sec late through York; but it was nothing to what we might have done if the engine had been given her head.

The Gateshead driver who had taken over at Newcastle was making his first trip on the train, and as the running of the 'Silver Jubilee' had been confined to Kings Cross men in both directions it would also have been his first on any of the streamlined trains. Chiefly from a tendency to over-emphasise the permanent speed restrictions he was running roughly 1 to $1\frac{1}{2}$min late from Selby to Grantham, but having climbed the 1 in 200 gradient up to Stoke summit at a minimum of $64\frac{1}{2}$mph he left the controls unchanged for the descent towards Peterborough. The result was not only a maximum speed of 106mph but an average for 10.3 miles of 104.3mph. This of course was thrilling beyond words for me, but one of my most lasting memories of it, is of the extreme smoothness of the riding of the coaches at what was then the highest speed I had ever logged in a train carrying fare-paying passengers. It was attained quite comfortably by the engine. There was no attempt to force her to a specially high speed. She was allowed to make her own pace, in violent contrast to the historic episode with *Mallard* a year later, when *driving* the latter engine to a rate of steam admission wildly outside normal practice led to the failure of the inside big end, admittedly after the world record had been made.

In the winter of 1938-9 there were two occasions in one week when slight defects on the booked A4 engine working down from Edinburgh made it necessary to change engines at Newcastle. The replacement in each case was an A3 with the regular driver and fireman who would have taken over in any case, Driver Nash and Fireman Gilbey, of Kings Cross. On the first occasion they had No 2595 *Trigo*, and made up 10 minutes on the schedule despite 5min loss by two speed restrictions. The net time for the 268.3 mile run was 225min, a brilliant average of $71\frac{1}{4}$mph, seeing that the engine had been commandeered at a moment's notice. Two days later they had engine No 2507 *Singapore*, and made even faster running. The actual time was $227\frac{1}{2}$min with the same permanent way slacks, leaving a net time of $222\frac{1}{2}$min — $72\frac{1}{4}$mph. They had the winter load of the train, namely 290 tons. There was an amusing sequel to these runs, told by my old chief

Capt Bernard H. Peter, Managing Director of the Westinghouse Brake and Signal Company. He was in some private discussions with Sir Nigel Gresley, when a secretary entered the room and handed the latter a memorandum. Gresley excused himself for a moment while he read the paper, and then a broad smile spread across his face. It was the report of *Singapore's* run, only two days after that of *Trigo*. He tossed the memorandum to his visitor saying: 'There you are, Peter; any of my damned engines can do the job, whether they have a tin case on or not!'

Top: The pioneer Gresley streamlined 4-6-2 No 2509 *Silver Link*, taking the 4.15pm semi-fast from Kings Cross to Peterborough, on Saturday 28 September 1935, two days before the inauguration of the 'Silver Jubilee' service between London and Newcastle.

Above: A scene at Leeds Central station in 1935: engines left to right are: ex-Manchester, Sheffield & Lincolnshire 0-6-2T of Parker design (vintage 1891-1901); ex-NER R class 4-4-0 (LNER Class D20); ex-GNR Atlantic No 4456, which has just backed down on to the 'Queen of Scots' Pullman, on which a record run to Kings Cross was recorded from the footplate by the author; a small ex-GNR 4-4-2T, and ex-GNR 0-6-0.

Above: The 'Royal Scot' on arrival at Euston, hauled by one of the Derby-built engines of the class No 6158 *The Loyal Regiment.*

Below: Euston-Manchester express near Carpenders Park in 1938, hauled by 3-cylinder 4-6-0 No 5552 *Silver Jubilee.*

Bottom: In the early days of the Stanier Pacifics: No 6201 *Princess Elizabeth* on arrival at Euston with the up 'Royal Scot'. The engine has worked through from Glasgow, and carries the traditional Caledonian semaphore route indicator on the smokebox door.

Top: The 'Coronation Scot' back in Euston, after the 'Invitation Run' from Euston to Crewe and return on 29 June, 1937, when a maximum speed of 114mph was attained.

Above: The first of the Garter blue A4s, No 4489 *Dominion of Canada*, introduced for haulage of the 'Coronation' streamliner. This photograph, taken at Kings Cross 'top shed', shows the engine before the Canadian bell was added at the front end.

Below: Kings Cross, top shed: engines being prepared. A4 4-6-2 No 4490 *Empire of India*, for the 'Coronation'; 2-6-2 No 4771 *Green Arrow* for the Scotch Goods, and Class K3 2-6-0 No 143 for another express goods train.

17
Finale: Grim Prospects Ahead

In those anxious months before the lamps of Europe went out for the second time in my lifetime, although preparations were urgently in hand to withstand the expected ordeal of all-out war the facade presented to the travelling public was of complete normality, and of continuing enterprise in passenger train services. I was concerned however with some of those preparations, kept carefully confidential, in case they should spread alarm at the seeming inevitability of war; and I was travelling more frequently to the Westinghouse works at Chippenham. As usual however I managed to combine some railway interest with journeys on professional duties, and I found that by getting up very early and catching the 7.30am breakfast car train from Paddington I could often conclude my work in time to catch the 3.38pm semi-fast *down* from Chippenham. This arrived in Bristol at 4.15pm, giving just a quarter of an hour to connect with the up 'Bristolian'. The 3.38pm down, which was the Weston-super-Mare section of the heavy, but lethargic 1.18pm from Paddington, usually ran on time, and I managed to get three runs back to London on the flyer.

With much signalling work on hand in the North Eastern Area of the LNER I was travelling frequently between Kings Cross and Darlington. I had a number of runs down on the 'Silver Jubilee', and as by that time the signalling between York and Northallerton had been converted the 4-aspect the 70mph speed limit no longer applied. Four runs can be summarised thus:

Engine	Load tons gross	Time to Darlington 232.3 miles Actual min sec	Net min	Av speed mph
Silver Link	235	195 10	191	73.0
Silver Link	290	200 05	195	71.5
Silver Fox	265	195 45	191	73.0
Dominion of New Zealand	265	195 10	$195\frac{1}{4}$	71.3

Schedule time was then 198min, and the variation in loading was due, first of all, to the use of one of the spare 'Coronation' sets, without the observation car, and then, on the last two runs, an extra-coach in the original 'Silver Jubilee' set.

My main interest at the time however was in the working of the A4 engines on heavy East Coast expresses. This originated on Saturdays when the Kings Cross engine and men of the down 'Silver Jubilee' on the Friday night returned from Newcastle on the up 'Flying Scotsman' and sometimes put up 'streamline' standards of running. The only trouble was that on Saturdays there was often a relief train running ahead of the 'Scotsman' from Newcastle. It naturally took the bulk of the local traffic, was heavy, and with a 'spare' non-streamlined Pacific to haul it, it got in the way of the 'Scotsman' proper. This was disappointing, especially south of Grantham, because it prevented keeping the sharp timing of 107min for the 105.5 miles to Kings Cross. On one particularly bad trip we were checked severely at Doncaster, and stopped dead at Newark, Huntingdon, and Potters Bar. On one of these runs, which had begun in brilliant style from Darlington, we had averaged 76.2mph from Northallerton to Beningbrough with a 530 ton train; on another we ran up to 80mph at Thirsk, in the teeth of a blizzard, only to be baulked of punctual running south of York by checks from the relief train.

I remember having some serious discussions with certain authorities at Kings Cross over the delays meted out to the 'Flying Scotsman' when the relief train was running. The relief ran non-stop from York to Kings Cross, and I suggested that once the relief had collected its load of passengers from York it could be routed via Knottingley, and follow the main train from Shaftholme Junction southwards. They agreed with me that late running of a train with the prestige of the 'Flying Scotsman' was a thoroughly bad thing, but in the spring of 1939 more weighty matters were concerning the operating department and the idea got no further. So far as collecting data of fast running was concerned, on more than one occasion I detrained from the 'Scotsman' at Grantham, and waited for the afternoon train from Edinburgh, leaving Grantham at 7.45pm. Although allowed 110min for that final 107.5 miles to Kings Cross I logged one run up in 102min, with a load of 515 tons and the A4 engine No 4900 then named *Gannet*.

While the facade of normality remained, and the recording of fast runs, and photography continued to give me much pleasure, I can recall no less vividly today how thin that facade was becoming. By the early summer of 1939 the flashpoint in central Europe had moved to Poland, doubly poignant for us in Westinghouse, because work on our tremendous contract for equipping the Polish State Railways with modern air brake equipment was nearing completion, and some of my friends were still resident in Warsaw. With France and Great Britain pledged to go to her aid in the event of an attack by the Axis powers every news bulletin was fraught with anxiety. Many a time when I arrived back in London after some visit to the north or west, I wondered if the evening papers would have news of the first shots in a campaign.

Despite the steadily worsening situation both the LMS and the LNER introduced improved services in May 1939, in the former's case including division of the morning Anglo-Scottish expresses into two parts in each direction. The non-stop time by these trains between Euston and Carlisle became 299min for 299.2 miles, and by this acceleration the LMS had, from May onwards, the remarkable aggregate of 6,880 miles daily scheduled at start-to-stop average speeds of 60mph and over. It was the Edinburgh portion of the up 'Royal Scot' that made this 60mph run up from Carlisle, and not long after its introduction I made an interesting journey joining the Aberdeen section at Stirling. It was worked by a 'Royal Scot' class engine, through to Carlisle. It consisted of no more than five coaches over this northernmost part of the journey; but the addition of the Edinburgh section at Symington made up the full load of 11, 339 tons tare, and with that the engine No 6102 *Black Watch* made an average speed of just over 60mph to Carlisle, 66.9 miles in 66¾min.

At Carlisle engines were changed, and another 'Royal Scot', No 6132 *The King's Regiment Liverpool* came on for the 299.2 mile non-stop 60mph run to

Euston. The start was punctual, and at first the engine was not pressed, taking $42\frac{1}{2}$min to pass Shap Summit, 31.4 miles, and 25min for the 31.4 miles down to Carnforth, with a maximum speed of $86\frac{1}{2}$mph. South of Preston, however, control had put in an excursion, between the Glasgow and Edinburgh sections of the 'Royal Scot'. This interloper was evidently not up to making an average speed of just over 60mph between Standish and Coppenhall Junctions, as we were scheduled to do, and the result was a whole series of signal checks, by which we lost $10\frac{3}{4}$min. Crewe was passed $10\frac{1}{2}$min late, and another check, not so severe, on the downhill run from Whitmore to Stafford suggested that even yet the road was not quite clear. When we passed Stafford we had only $115\frac{1}{2}$min left for the remaining 133.6 miles, if we were to make a punctual arrival in Euston. Allowing for the usual run-in time from Willesden Junction we had $107\frac{1}{2}$min, for 128.2 miles — an average of 71.7mph. This was 'Cheltenham Flyer', or 'Coronation' speed with a load of 355 tons, and in the latter comparison a 'Royal Scot' instead of an A4.

By the way we recovered from the Stafford speed restriction however, and tore into it across the Trent Valley it was evident that our driver was determined to do it; and from being 10min late after the last signal check the arrears were reduced to 8min, at Tamworth, 6min at Nuneaton, $3\frac{1}{4}$min at Rugby, 1min at Bletchley, and $\frac{1}{2}$min *early* at Tring. The 77.5 miles from Rugeley to Bletchley, scheduled in 71min, took only $62\frac{1}{2}$min, and by that time the driver was getting things so well in hand that he could begin to ease up a little. After a final 82mph down the fast descent from Tring, and passing Watford $1\frac{1}{4}$min early, he steamed the engine very lightly indeed. With a beautifully judged finish we stopped in Euston $\frac{1}{2}$min early — 298min, 33sec, to be exact from Carlisle. The really hard spell from Rugeley to Bletchley, where we averaged 75mph and regained $8\frac{1}{2}$min, included the slack through Rugby, to 38mph and to appreciate the vigour of the locomotive work one needs to study the averages from Colwich to Rugby No 7 Box (just before the slack) 43.8 miles, and from Welton to Leighton Buzzard, 35.1 miles. These two stretches were covered at average speeds of 77.3 and 78.5mph respectively, both including a fair amount of 'give and take' in the gradients, and including maximum speeds of $86\frac{1}{2}$ and 88mph.

It was a magnificent piece of running, all the more commendable in that the driver went really hard to regain the lost time as quickly as he could, and get his train running once again in its correct timetable path; but having done so he completely eschewed any attempts at a spectacular finish, and bringing the train considerably ahead of time. With a continuation of the previous effort I estimate he could not have cut at least 4min, more off the overall time, leaving a possible net time of 282min, for the 299.2 miles from Carlisle, and an average speed throughout of 63.6mph. It was one of the last long distance runs I had on the LMS before the fatal September of 1939 and it was indeed a stirring memory to take into the dark years that followed.

With the blackout curtains drawn, and passenger train speeds at first limited to a maximum of 45mph, start-to-stop, one fell inevitably to looking back on the period between the wars, and to recalling all that had been achieved. The earlier years had been spent recovering to somewhere near the standards that had been attained by 1914. Then, despite the great depression, and the straitened finances of all the British railways, the standards of train service had gone notably ahead, and it is always fascinating to try and imagine how things might have developed still further if war had not come. Financially all the British railways were operating on a shoe string, severely handicapped by legislation that had become out of date. Furthermore the campaign launched in the winter of 1938-9 urging a 'Square Deal' for the railways, and for the removal of restrictions, so far as the fixing of rates and fares were concerned that handicapped them severely in competing with road haulage, got a very bad press. Public opinion was not sympathetic to railways. In motive power both Gresley and Stanier had designs outlined for larger express passenger locomotives, Gresley for a huge 3-cylinder 4-8-2, looking like an elongated version of an A3 Pacific, while Stanier was contemplating a 4-6-4, version of the streamlined 'Coronation' class. In 1939 neither the LMS nor the LNER seemed to envisage a general change to diesel or electric traction for long distance main line work, although preparations for the Manchester-Sheffield-Wath electrification scheme on the LNER were well advanced when war broke out.

In 1941 there came developments which showed the way things might have progressed on the LNER and which gave a foretaste of what did eventuate on the Southern. The saga of the 'Merchant Navy' and 'West Country' Pacifics is well known, but on the LNER things went far otherwise from what Gresley had in mind. Even before the outbreak of war the most obvious need for development on that railway was in medium power locomotives to replace the ageing collection of Atlantics and 4-6-0s inherited from the pre-Grouping companies, and with his firm adherence to 3-cylinder propulsion, and the need to provide a design having a very high route availability the two prototype V4 2-6-2 mixed traffic engines were built at Doncaster. It was a powerful engine, with a nominal tractive effort of 27,420lb and able to run over 5,000 out of the total route mileage of 6,414 on the LNER. There is no doubt that Gresley envisaged bulk building of these engines, in due course; but his death, shortly after the first of them had been completed altered the entire situation, and no more V4s were built. The change in policy that followed was as perplexing to many of the men on the line as it was to countless enthusiasts who had been devoted to Gresley's products; but the change, no less than that which was beginning on the Southern, marked September 1939 as the end of an era in yet another sense, alongside the gigantic upheaval that engulfed the nations of Western Europe.

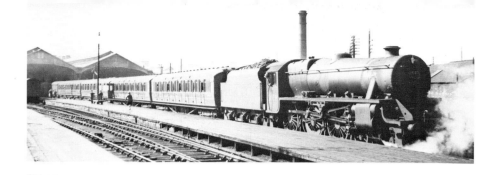

Left: One of the first four streamlined A4s to have twin-orifice blastpipes and double chimneys: No 4902 *Seagull* leaving Grantham with the 1.20pm Kings Cross to Edinburgh.

Top: Aberdeen express (LNER stock) ready to leave Inverness, hauled by Stanier 'Black Five' 4-6-0 No 5018 in 1939.

Above: The Stanier 2-6-4Ts on the London commuter service: No 2494 on a Euston train at Watford Junction.

Below: Stanier small 2-6-2T No 188, at Blair Atholl, working on Perth-Blair Atholl local trains.

Top: 'Black Fives' on the Callander and Oban line: 4-6-0 No 5362 at Balquhidder on the evening Glasgow to Oban express.

Above: One of the 3-cylinder 2-6-0s of Class K4 No 3443 *Cameron of Lochiel* on up West Highland goods at Crianlarich.

Below: Last weeks before the war: the A4 4-6-2 No 4487 *Sea Eagle* leaving York, on the 1.20pm Kings Cross to Edinburgh express in late August 1939.